Metal Detectin

The Ultimate Guide to all the Best Places to make Great Finds

David Villanueva

ISBN-13: 9798498703640

DEDICATION

To Helen

CONTENTS

ACKNOWLEDGMENTS

Several images are reused in this book, with grateful thanks, under various Creative Commons Licences. To view copies of these licences, visit http://creativecommons.org/licenses/ or send a letter to Creative Commons, 171 Second Street, Suite 300, San Francisco, California, 94105, USA.

I would like to thank all who have so generously made their work freely available on line at Wikipedia.org, and elsewhere.

1 INTRODUCTION

Over more than two thousand years, literally many millions of coins and metal artefacts have been lost, mislaid or buried on land and in water. Armed with a metal detector you can find your share and armed with this book you can make your share much larger.

All places you might search are not equal and if you habitually search places where nothing much happened in the past then your finds bag will contain nothing much. A good site for metal detecting is one that has seen use by at least a few people over a long period of time, or has been used briefly by many. But there are other important factors such as the user being of a time and wealthy enough to have metal items to lose, as well as virtually unused places being littered with finds through waste disposal. Everywhere there have been areas of human activity and natural events significant enough to bury or sink metal artefacts and offer great potential reward.

This is a book of leads to the type of site that will likely produce worthwhile results, together with resources for you to follow-up to find such sites in your own area. You may have to carry out a little research but in many cases it will require nothing more than looking at a map. Whatever places you choose to search you should endeavour to build a portfolio of different types of site that will potentially allow you to metal detect throughout the year. And again, this book will lead you to those sites.

Before we get started, I should point out that every sport or recreational activity has its rules and metal detecting is no exception, so lets get that out of the way and then we can get on with the fun stuff.

Firstly, there are a number of laws affecting ownership of what we find and these are covered in the section on Treasure Law below. Secondly, all land is owned by someone so you can't just go metal detecting anywhere you like – you need to obtain permission from the landowner. However, any land you own and public beaches are generally OK to metal detect on providing there are no legal restraints.

While searching beaches and tidal rivers is not everyone's idea of fun, they are places where you can generally metal detect either without the formality of obtaining permission or, in some cases, you can buy a permit to search. While, there are many beaches and tidal river foreshores in private ownership, the usual 'ownership' in Britain is Local Authority above high water mark and Crown below.

The Crown now grants a permissive right to metal detect which will effectively cover all foreshore in England, Northern Ireland, Scotland and Wales under their control. The foreshore is defined as: the area between mean high and mean low water of ordinary tides (spring tides in Scotland). The terms and conditions of this arrangement and be obtained from their website: https://www.thecrownestate.co.uk/media/2762/terms-and-conditions-of-metal-detecting.pdf Maps showing Crown foreshore in many areas can also be downloaded from the website.

In Scotland, everyone has a statutory right of access to beaches, foreshores and the countryside in general for outdoor pursuits, apparently including responsible metal detecting, so no permit is necessary. There are obviously a number of restrictions such as cultural heritage and archaeological sites so check out the Scottish Outdoor Access Code: http://www.outdooraccess-scotland.com/outdoors-responsibly/your-access-rights/

In the case of the river Thames, the Port of London Authority effectively owns the foreshore and runs a three-year permit system, backdated to the preceding 1st of January (unless applied for or renewed between December and January), for metal detecting between Teddington and the Thames Barrier. The current fee is £55.00 (day permit: £20). See the National Council for Metal Detecting Website: http://www.ncmd.co.uk/ for conditions and an application form. Applications to: Mr K Jackelman, Port of London of Authority, London River House, Royal Pier Road, GRAVESEND, Kent DA12 2BG. Tel: 01474 562339. Email: foreshorepermits@pla.co.uk

Public beaches are usually accessible for metal detecting. There may be local bylaws however, which must be adhered to for the sake of the hobby. Bylaws will usually restrict detecting to early mornings and evenings during the holiday season. This is for the benefit of all beach users and, whether bylaws exist or not, you shouldn't be searching with a metal detector around sunbathers and others enjoying the beach, unless you have been asked specifically to find some newly lost property. It is just bad manners as well as being a very inefficient way to search.

Private beaches where the public has free access are usually equally accessible for metal detecting as the public variety, (although strictly you should seek permission from the owner). In many cases you won't be able to tell the difference. However, do look out for notices, which may affect access or searching. Private, Keep Out, means just that, unless you obtain permission and bear in mind the restriction may be because of danger. Ministry of Defence (MOD) property is a case in point. Some beaches and foreshores are designated Sites of Special Scientific Interest (SSSI) and while pedestrian access may be allowed, metal detecting may be prohibited. The National Trust (or regional equivalents) owns quite a number of beaches and will not usually allow metal detecting without a good reason. However, they will seldom own the entire beach and foreshore so it is quite possible to work around their area of ownership, provided you find out from e.g. Ordnance Survey maps what area they own. Some hotels own beaches for the enjoyment of their guests. You may be able to gain permission out-of-season and you could offer to search for guests' lost property in-season.

The situation with non-tidal waterways or watercourses is somewhat different. A landowner with a frontage along a watercourse is presumed to own the bed up to the centre of the watercourse. Obviously if the same landowner owns both banks then he owns the entire bed. Unless there is proof to the contrary. Sometimes errors in land deals occur and the bed is not transferred with the land, sometimes beds are bought and sold separately. The usual case with working canals and some rivers is that ownership is vested in the navigation authority by Act of Parliament to facilitate control over the use of the waterway.

While detecting non-tidal watercourses does require permission from the landowner, notwithstanding the rights of other users such as anglers, permission may be easier to obtain than that on the surrounding land. Not only that, like beaches and foreshores, watercourses are potentially a year round site and benefit from replenishment.

From Natural England's booklet: **Out in the country,** (2007) page 25, which can be downloaded free at:

http://publications.naturalengland.org.uk/publication/9027

"You may carry and use a metal detector on a right of way. But you are not permitted to disturb the ground in order to remove anything, without the landowner's permission. To do so may be trespass, criminal damage, or theft. This prohibition also applies to beaches. It is also an offence to use a metal detector on the site of a scheduled monument or area of archaeological importance in order to find objects of historical or archaeological interest without written permission from the Secretary of State for Communities and Local Government.

Public rights of access to open access areas do not extend to taking a metal detector with you or using it. The National Council for Metal Detecting publishes a code of conduct for detector users."

This is interesting since you clearly can use a metal detector on any public right of way to which pedestrians have access, providing you only remove surface finds. You can check out rights of way for potential targets to see if a search may be worthwhile before you seek permission to dig. Ownership is much the same as a watercourse. If you carry this out, be prepared for the landowner to approach you; leave digging tools behind and carry a copy of the booklet to show them and hopefully you will be able to sort out permission on the spot.

The code of practice following, is basically voluntary but there are some legal requirements and much common sense included so it would be a good idea to follow the code as closely as you can even if you live outside of England and Wales.

Code of Practice for Responsible Metal Detecting in England & Wales (2017 Revision)

If undertaken responsibly metal-detecting can make an important contribution to archaeological knowledge. This document aims to provide guidance for metal-detectorists who wish to contribute to our understanding of the history of England and Wales. It combines both the requirements of finders under the law, as well as more general voluntary guidance on accepted best practice.

Being responsible means:

Before you go metal-detecting

*1 Not trespassing; before you start detecting obtain permission to search from the landowner, regardless of the status, or perceived status, of the land. Remember that all land (including parks, public open-spaces, beaches and foreshores) has an owner and an occupier (such as a tenant farmer) can only grant permission with both the landowner's and tenant's agreement. Any finds discovered will normally be the property of the landowner, so to avoid disputes it is advisable to get permission and agreement in writing first regarding the ownership of any finds subsequently discovered.

*2 Obeying the law concerning protected sites (such as those defined as Scheduled Monuments, Sites of Special Scientific Interest or military crash sites, and those involving human remains), and also those other sites on which metal-detecting might also be restricted (such as land under Countryside Stewardship or other agri-environment schemes). You can obtain details of these sites from several sources, including the landowner/ occupier, your local Finds Liaison Officer or Historic Environment Record or at:

http://www.magic.gov.uk / https://historicengland.org.uk/listing/the-list/ http://www.cadw.gov.wales

— which will help research and better understand the site. Take extra care when detecting near protected sites since it is not always clear where the boundaries of these lie on the ground.

*3 Familiarising yourself with the Portable Antiquities Scheme (including contact details for your local Finds Liaison Officer — see https://finds.org.uk / 0207 323 8611), and its guidance on the recording of archaeological finds discovered by the public; make it clear to the landowner that you wish to record finds with the Portable Antiquities Scheme. Ensure that you follow current conservation advice on the handling, care and storage of archaeological objects (see https://finds.org.uk/conservation/index).

*4 Obtaining public liability insurance (to protect yourself and others from accidental damage), such as that offered by the National Council for Metal Detecting or the Federation of Independent Detectorists.

While you are metal-detecting

*5 Working on ground that has already been disturbed (such as ploughed land or that which has formerly been ploughed), and only within the depth of ploughing. If detecting takes place on pasture, be careful to ensure that no damage is done to the archaeological value of the land, including earthworks. Avoid damaging stratified archaeological deposits (that is to say, finds that seem to be in the place where they were deposited in antiquity) and minimise any ground disturbance through the use of suitable tools and by reinstating any ground and turf as neatly as possible.

*6 Stopping any digging and making the landowner aware that you are seeking expert help if you discover something below the ploughsoil, or a concentration of finds or unusual material, or wreck remains. Your local Finds Liaison Officer may be able to help or will be able to advise on an appropriate person. Reporting the find does not change your rights of discovery, but will result in far more archaeological evidence being recovered.

*7 Recording findspots as accurately as possible for all archaeological finds (i.e. to at least a one ten metre square — an 8-Figure National Grid Reference), using a hand-held Global Positioning Systems (GPS) device whilst in the field or a 1:25000 scale map if this is not possible. Bag finds individually, recording the National Grid Reference on the bag with a waterproof/indelible marker. Archaeologists are interested in learning about all archaeological finds you discover, not just metallic items, because such finds contribute to knowledge.

*8 Respecting the Country Code (leave gates and property as you find them and do not damage crops, frighten animals, or disturb ground nesting birds, and dispose properly of litter; see:

https://www.gov.uk/government/publications/the-countryside-code (You may also like to get a copy of the more extensive *Out in the country* booklet from Natural England:

http://publications.naturalengland.org.uk/publication/79046)

After you have been metal-detecting

*9 Reporting all archaeological finds to the relevant landowner/occupier; and making it clear to the landowner that you wish to record archaeological finds to the Portable Antiquities Scheme, so the information can pass into the local Historic Environment Record. Both the Country Land and Business Association and the National Farmers Union support the reporting of finds with the Portable Antiquities Scheme. Details of your local Finds Liaison Officer can be found at see https://finds.org.uk/contacts / e-mail info@finds.org.uk or phone 0207 323 8611.

*10 Abiding by the statutory provisions of the Treasure Act 1996, the Treasure Act Code of Practice https://finds.org.uk/treasure and wreck law

https://www.gov.uk/government/organisations/maritime-and-coastguard-agency If you wish to take artefacts and archaeological material older than 50 years old out of the UK, you will require an export licence http://www.artscouncil.org.uk/export-controls/export-licensing If you need advice your local Finds Liaison Officer will be able to help you.

*11 Calling the Police (101), and notifying the landowner/occupier, if you find any traces of human remains or a likely burial; human remains can only be disturbed further with a Ministry of Justice licence https://www.gov.uk/apply-for-an-exhumation-licence

*12 Calling the Police or HM Coastguard, and notifying the landowner/occupier, if you find anything that may be a live explosive,

device or other ordnance. Do not attempt to move or interfere with any such explosives.

*13 Calling the Police if you notice any illegal activity whilst out metal-detecting, such as theft of farm equipment or illegal metal-detecting (nighthawking). Further details can be found by contacting Historic England/Cadw or the 'heritage crime' contact within your local police force.

While I do not pretend to be a lawyer, there are a number of legal definitions that could apply to metal detecting finds together with the popular court ruling on finds made under each category:

Lost property, which has been involuntarily parted from its owner, belongs to the owner or their heirs and if they cannot be traced, title goes to the finder. You are legally obliged to take reasonable steps to return lost property to its owner. In the case of loose change it is highly unlikely you will find an owner, so that is yours to keep. Recently a woman received a fine and a criminal record for theft because she found and kept a £20 note on the floor of a shop. If you find a large sum of money or a piece of jewelry, for example, you could report it to the local police, if lost property is in their remit, or take suitable action to find the owner such as advertising in a local newspaper or on social media. The police generally disclaim lost property after one month. Although recently, as the police do not have a statutory duty to deal with lost property, some forces are no longer accepting lost property so, as long as you can show you have made reasonable attempts to trace the owner, it is yours to keep unless it may be evidence of a crime, is dangerous, illegal (e.g. an offensive weapon) or contains personal information. Reasonable steps to trace the owner nowadays usually involves social media such as neighbourhood groups and providing you do that and wait a month or so, the find is technically yours. Bear in mind that the owner retains all rights to their property, so if he or she turns up later then they can still legally demand its return or all proceeds if the item has been sold. The owner may offer you a reward for returning their property but is under no obligation to do so and you would be committing an offence if you refuse to hand the property back unless a reward is paid. The joy expressed when you hand back lost jewelry is reward enough in itself. In Britain, if you find paper money which is unfit for circulation, the Bank of England will usually be able to replace it. Take any banknotes to your local bank in the first instance for advice.

Mislaid property, where the owner puts the object down and forgets about it, reverts to the site owner, if not claimed by the owner.

Abandoned property, which is simply thrown away, goes to the finder.

Embedded property refers to buried artefacts or even natural minerals, which fall outside the definition of treasure trove and if the owner or heirs cannot be traced, belong to the landowner. As such you need an agreement with the landowner over disposal of finds.

Archaeological objects or portable antiquities may cover excavated objects as recent as 50 years old. Except for treasure items, reporting in the UK is only mandatory in Scotland, where all excavated objects are treasure and a reward is paid for retained items. Voluntary reporting is encouraged in the rest of the UK for non-treasure items. Export licenses may be required before such objects can be removed from the country.

Treasure trove, defined as objects, less than 300 years old, made substantially of gold, silver and their alloys (plus paper money) hidden or concealed for several decades, with the intention of recovery, where the owners or heirs cannot be traced. Treasure trove is now incorporated in the Treasure Act in England and Wales, although paper money is excluded. Treasure is normally shared equally between land or site owner and finder. If the finder was trespassing then finds go to the landowner or site owner. Finds on government land go to the government unless there is a prior agreement in place.

Wreck, being an abandoned vessel (including aircraft), or something abandoned off a vessel, which is afloat, stranded, aground or sunken. The salvager is normally entitled to a reward related to the value of the find. Wreck that we find, for the most part, will be washed up or buried on a beach. Deciding what is wreck is mainly a matter of common sense but if you are unsure, contact your Finds Liaison Officer for advice or report it anyway. Further information is available from: https://www.gov.uk/guidance/wreck-and-salvage-law

The Treasure Act in Britain

At present, treasure is defined, under the Act, as any object other than a coin, at least 300 years old when found, which has a metallic content, of which at least 10% by weight is gold or silver. And all coins that contain at least 10% by weight of gold or silver that come from the same find consisting of at least two coins, at least 300 years old. And all coins that contain less than 10% by weight gold or silver that come from the same find consisting of at least ten coins at least 300 years old. And any associated objects, except un-worked natural objects (e.g. a pot or other container), found in the same place as treasure objects. And any objects or coin hoards less than 300 years old, made substantially of gold and silver that have been deliberately hidden with the intention of recovery and for which the owner is unknown. Since 1 January 2003 the definition of treasure has been extended on prehistoric (i.e. up to the end of the Iron

Age) finds to include all multiple artifacts, made of any metal, found together and single artifacts deliberately containing any quantity of precious metal.

The Act applies to objects found anywhere in England, Wales and Northern Ireland, including in or on land, in buildings (whether occupied or ruined), in rivers and lakes and on the foreshore (the area between mean high water and mean low water) providing the object does not come from a wreck.

If you are searching in other parts of the British Isles or outside of Britain altogether, you should familiarize yourself with treasure law and the laws on metal detecting, for your specific area. In Scotland, for instance, all ownerless objects belong to the Crown. They must be reported regardless of where they were found or of what they are made. The finder receives market value as long as no laws have been broken. Not all finds will be claimed. Further information from: Treasure Trove Unit, National Museum of Scotland, Chambers Street, Edinburgh, EH1 1JF.

I have the experience of having had to report over a dozen separate finds of treasure since the introduction of the Treasure Act. While there were concerns over lack of confidentiality regarding the find spot in the early days, everything has settled down, generally working well and fairly to all parties involved. I still urge you to be cautious when reporting your finds, so here are my unofficial suggestions for protecting yourself and your landowner friends when you find potential treasure:

* Leave your treasure 'as found' and resist all temptation to clean or restore your find except for the absolute minimum necessary to identify it as possible treasure.

* The National Council for Metal Detecting will willingly advise in the process of reporting treasure and it is well worth involving them from the start when you have possible treasure to report.

* County Finds Liaison Officers (FLOs) are now heavily involved in the treasure process and will also advise and help.

* Your only legal obligation is to report the finding of potential treasure to the Coroner within fourteen days of becoming aware that it is possibly treasure.

* Discuss the matter with the landowner as soon as possible.

* Do the reporting yourself. The legal responsibility for reporting rests with the finder and no one will look after your interests as well as you.

* Bear in mind, especially if you want to keep the coin, that the first coin found of a scattered hoard may not be treasure, if it was the only coin found on that occasion and there was sufficient time to sell the coin before the finding of the second coin.

* Report your find to the Coroner in writing within 14 days and keep a copy of the letter. In the first instance only report the find spot as the name of the parish in which the find was made. If it is not clear which Coroner needs to be informed, ask your FLO or write to the most likely Coroner and ask for your letter to be passed on, as necessary. In my area it is current practice for finds to be reported to the FLO in lieu of the Coroner. As this is not strictly the letter of the law, I report to the Coroner in writing and send a copy to the FLO.

* Always take photographs or have photographs taken of all possible views of all objects, before you hand the objects over. You will at least have something to show an independent valuation expert and, if you want to publish, there will not be any copyright or access issues.

* There is no time limit for handing over the find and you should be allowed a reasonable amount of time for such things as photographing, valuing, showing it to the landowner, displaying it at a club meeting etc. Bear in mind, however, that you are responsible for the security of the find until you hand it over.

* These days Finds Liaison Officers often collect potential treasure from finders; however you may be asked to deposit your find at a museum or FLO at your own expense. You are not legally obliged to take your find anywhere, however, if you can arrange this it is best to comply. Insist on being given the Treasure Receipt, (filled out in your presence) in exchange for your find.

* The Treasure Act Code of Practice requires that the precise find spot must be established and should be kept confidential. You can insist on the confidentiality requirement when the Treasure Receipt is completed and have the precise find spot kept separately.

* A section of the Treasure Receipt is labeled 'Location of find spot'. Only enter vague details of the find spot such as name of Parish, four-figure map reference or a nondescript site name such as 'Field A'.

* If a museum is interested in acquiring the find, a Coroner's Inquest will be arranged. You should be invited to attend the Inquest for which you can claim expenses and I suggest you should attend if you possibly can – you will at least know who was there and what was said. The press may be there, so be careful not to reveal find spot information if they are.

* Following an Inquest the Press will probably want to speak to you. Whether you speak to them is up to you but you can at least appeal for some confidentiality and perhaps avoid them uncovering, or inventing, more than you would like revealed.

* The final stumbling block is the valuation, which will be given via the Department for Culture Media and Sport some weeks after the Inquest. You need to know if the valuation is 'A Fair Market Value' so that you can decide whether to accept it. Fair market value is an attempt to arrive at the price you should expect to get if selling your find on the open market and the Treasure Valuation Committee tries to arrive at the 'hammer' price without auctioneer's deductions. Pick out a couple of dealers specializing in coins or objects similar to yours from the advertisements in treasure hunting magazines. Ask the dealers to give you their buying-in price for your find (send photographs if necessary). I am sure they will oblige for little or no charge. If the treasure is very rare it should be possible to arrange viewing for independent appraisal. You should be offered two opportunities to contest the valuation, one before the valuation committee meets and one after. I would accept the valuation if it falls within or above your dealers' ballpark figures and contest it if it falls below. If you are going to contest the valuation, get in before the committee meets if you can. There is a slight possibility that the museum involved may contest the valuation and succeed in getting it reduced – if this happens, unless there is clear justification, you could appeal against it all the way to the Secretary of State, if necessary.

* An alternative is for you or the landowner or both to refuse any award for the find when you first report it or at any time, preferably prior to any inquest. The find will then be offered to interested museums at a 50% or 100% discount depending, if one or both parties refuse the award.

2 AGRICULTURE

On farmland you seldom get the opportunity to completely cover anything other than the odd small area of arable land or larger areas under grass. Most fields used to be ploughed annually, ensuring a new crop of finds each year and land was left for relatively long periods before drilling, allowing searching for several months. Today, economic pressures on farming have reduced ploughing to a minimum, drilling of new seed taking place a few days after harvesting from the back of a cultivator. Now there's a new game afoot – direct drilling into stubble! The result is a much shorter detecting season on farmland. And if you detected from dawn to dusk you would be unlikely to thoroughly cover so much as an acre. So, unless your research or landscape observation has indicated certain areas will be more worthwhile than others, detecting tends to be very much a matter of sampling. On ploughed fields, when you do find something of interest you should search a very large area around the location. Modern cultivation distributes soil, stones and other objects far and wide. Look carefully also for pieces of china, pottery, or oyster shells since any of these often have metal objects in amongst them.

Metal detector technology is constantly improving and objects not found some years ago could very easily be found today with a modern detector. Even if you or someone else has searched an area before, providing the site has potential, you should try again. Soil conditions are always changing and the last person who searched may have not been as thorough as you will be. No metal detectorist ever finds everything and you may have a better technique or a different detector to the one used by searchers before you.

If you know how farming works you can maximise your searching of farmland and make finds throughout most of the year. The farmland of

Britain is basically divided into about two-thirds grassland for animals and one-third arable land for crops. The West tends to be under grass and the East arable, with rainfall tending to be the defining factor. Always bear in mind that the farm produces the farmer's livelihood and do nothing that may interfere with that. Always come to an agreement (usually a 50/50 split and preferably in writing) about what is to happen to your finds and providing the item is not potential treasure, always give way if the farmer fancies a particular find, regardless of any agreement. The farmer may want you to call in each time you visit to check it is convenient for you to detect in a particular field and again when you have finished to show your finds, even if he says you can keep them all. Farmers are always busy, so don't outstay your welcome. As far as you are concerned, whatever the farmer says you can or cannot do on the farm, is law. Some farmers will be happy to let you detect on some crops, such as cereals, that are knee high, while others will want you off the field as soon as it is drilled. If you just accept and do what the farmer says, without argument, then you won't go far wrong and I'm sure it will not be long before you and your farmer become firm friends.

Lets take a look at arable land on which crops are regularly planted in the ground. There is a considerable variety of crops grown and I will only have room for generalisations here, so I advise you to do at least a little research on agriculture in your area. Most arable crops have both Winter (sown in the Autumn) and Spring sown varieties, while others, like root crops, are grown on a rotational basis for harvesting throughout the year. If a farmer is going to be sowing a spring crop, it is quite likely the field will be ploughed in the Autumn and left in this state until the Spring, for the frost to break down the soil, particularly on heavy or clay soils. In Spring there should be a couple of weeks after the crop has been drilled when the land will be flat and perfect for metal detecting, providing you are allowed on that land, of course. So, it is worth asking your farmer friends if they are leaving any land to over-winter for Spring sowing and asking them what crops are being sown and when.

Growing and climate conditions can make a difference of several weeks to the time crops are ready to harvest. Of the commonly grown grain and seed crops, Winter rape is usually harvested in late July or early August, followed by cereals, such as barley, oats and wheat and then peas and beans during August to September when maize and linseed are usually the last crops harvested. Once the crop has been harvested some sort of stubble will usually be left (pea stubble is almost none existent). Cereal crops tend to have very short stubble as the stalks are cut for straw for animal feed or perhaps fuel. The oilseeds and bean stalks are usually left around a foot (30cm) high, which makes detecting over them quite a challenge. If you are lucky the farmer may mow or disk them to make it easier for him to plough or cultivate the stubble back in to the ground. The problem with fresh stubble is it is difficult to push the detector search head through it and so you effectively lose detection depth. Maize is planted in rows around 30 inches (76cm) apart so you can detect in between the growing plants (with care and farmer's consent) and the stubble after harvest. Stubble left for a few weeks soon starts to rot and softens up until it eventually becomes almost as easy as searching over grass.

Root crops like carrots, potatoes and turnips can be harvested throughout the year, while brassicas like, cabbage, cauliflower and sprouts can be harvested between July and October or even later. Some varieties of turnip are planted in Autumn to provide animal fodder in the ground over winter. The animals, particularly sheep, are fenced in to graze off the crop in strips leaving bare ground on which you can usually detect.

There have been subsidy schemes for farmers for a good number of years, which often result in many arable acres being left uncultivated for months or years. There is still a sort of 'set-aside' as it used to be called, where a field is left for the birds after harvest until the following Spring, when it will be sprayed off with a weedkiller and then cultivated and drilled with a new crop. Under the latest scheme in England, Countryside Stewardship, signed-up farmers will be leaving wide strips uncultivated around the edges of their arable fields, which might mean more detecting land.

Then there is fruit growing. Fruit trees such as apple, cherry and pear are usually planted in rows in orchards with a grass strip in between rows. Much soft fruit like blackcurrents, gooseberries and raspberries grow on bushes or canes and are usually laid out similarly to fruit trees, although the rows will be closer together. Apples and pears are usually picked or harvested in September or October, while soft fruits tend to be harvested throughout the Summer months. Once harvesting is finished, orchards should be available to search round to the following Spring when the blossom starts to appear, although there will be a short intermission during pruning. You can usually search both the bare earth around trees and bushes, (just be careful not to damage the roots on young stock) as well as the regularly mown grass strips. Once the blossom starts to appear it is probably a good idea to cease searching until after harvest so you avoid damaging the crop and also getting stung by bees, which are introduced into orchards to encourage pollination.

Grassland or pasture is very common in Britain and used basically for feeding farm animals. Some grass fields are grazed short by animals, while other fields are left to grow, animal free, and are mown a couple of times a year to produce hay or silage for feeding the animals during the winter months, when grass doesn't grow so well and the animals are often kept inside. Pasture offers plenty of opportunity for detecting in the winter months, when the grass is generally short and free of animals. Of course if the ground is frozen it will be difficult or impossible to dig finds out and on snow covered ground you will lose detection depth equivalent to the depth of snow. The only snow covered places possibly worth searching (for recent losses) are ski slopes and toboggan runs.

In warmer times of the year grassland for producing hay or silage will be searchable for a few weeks after mowing. Grazing land is searchable most of the year providing the farmer is happy to let you loose in amongst his animals. You also need to be comfortable detecting with grazing animals around you and to be very careful to fill your holes properly to avoid injured animals. If a horse or cow breaks a leg it usually has to be shot. Detecting with sheep is rarely a problem, they are timid creatures and tend to keep out of your way, unless they fancy that your finds bag contains food for them. Cows and calves tend to be inquisitive so you need to keep one eye on them while detecting; sometimes they'll completely ignore you and at other times the entire herd will come and see what you are up to. This can be a problem as they are large animals and unpredictably may jump around or even stampede, so if they get too close get out of their way or out of that particular field. And never ever detect in a field containing a bull. Horses are usually grazed alone or in small numbers in paddocks of just a few acres. Horses can kick and bite so you really need to know what the horse's temperament is before detecting with them. Likewise there are other creatures you may encounter, such as pigs, goats, llamas and rheas, which you'll need to take advice from the farmer before detecting among them.

There are two other issues with grassland that you need to be aware of. One is that in hot weather the ground can become very hard and dry. Finds become difficult to dig out and no matter how careful you reinstate the ground, the grass will die off leaving unsightly patches where you have been digging, holes can even reform if the dead grass gets kicked out by animals. You can mitigate this by dragging a considerable quantity of water around with you and watering the grass, you have removed, back into the ground but is it worth the effort? The other issue is that on permanent grassland you will be up against the law of diminishing returns on the finds you make, since metal objects sink and other than the action of burrowing animals, there is nothing to bring them back up into the surface layers. Once a pasture field stops producing, the only way you will get more finds out of it is to search with a deeper-seeking metal detector.

There are a number of agricultural features worth looking out for:

Banks of the earthen variety are well worth searching for possible hoards or caches.

Barns see much activity and as well as searching outside will repay searching inside if they have earth or wood floors.

Boundary walls. People sit against them and they are also used for markers.

Chicken coups are regularly attended for collecting eggs and feeding chickens.

Earthworks such as ditches and mounds (check they are not scheduled ancient monuments).

Fence posts. Hoards have been found under or at the side of posts; corner posts in particular act as a good marker.

Fruit-Picking Fields such as those growing strawberries see a lot of activity and finger rings often get lost here.

Gates see activity in opening and closing. Produce is often sold at main gates, milk churns were collected and delivered, etc. Ornamental gateways are usually the remains of manor estates.

Hedges as well as their prime functions of boundaries and to keep farm animals from straying, have been used for burying hoards, shelter, provision of nuts, berries and wood among other uses. The older the hedge the more use it will have seen. A rough guide to estimating the age of a hedge is to count the number of different woody species in a 30m stretch and multiply by 100 years.

Hop Gardens. For about a century, 5,000 hop-pickers were employed for three to four weeks annually, on one 300-acre farm. Can you imagine the metal losses that would have occurred? This was one of the most famous Kent hop farms and at the peak of the hop growing industry in the 1870s, a temporary workforce of around a quarter of a million people were pouring into hop farms around the UK every September.

While Kent produced around one-third of Britain's hops, several other counties, notably Essex, Gloucestershire, Hampshire, Herefordshire, Hertfordshire, Nottinghamshire, Shropshire, Suffolk, Surrey, Sussex and Worcestershire were responsible for the other two-thirds.

How did this phenomenon come about? Ale, originally an alcoholic beverage brewed from fermented malt without hops, has been produced in Britain since at least Roman times. Ale's pleasant effects, when consumed in moderation, were secondary to its original purpose, which was to provide a relatively safe liquid intake when much of British water, particularly in towns, wasn't safe to drink. Ale didn't keep well and so brewing was very much a home industry with most households and every inn producing their own beverages.

Immigrants from the Low Countries, now Belgium and Holland, introduced their beer brewed with hops into Britain in around 1400. Naturally, the brew was resisted as a Protestant drink being foisted on a Catholic nation and hops in beer were blamed for Jack Cade's 1450 rebellion. However, beer had a great advantage over traditional ale as the hops acted as a preservative, therefore the brew kept longer and could be transported, giving the brewer a potentially much larger market.

By the beginning of the sixteenth century, beer was becoming popular and was encouraged by Edward VI. By the end of the seventeenth century commercial breweries had almost entirely replaced inn brewing.

The hops were originally supplied from the Continent until the sixteenth century when Kent started growing hops to supply the flourishing brewing industry. Good soil, enclosed fields, ample wood for poles and charcoal for drying the hops made Kent ideal for the purpose.

Much labour was required for the hop harvest; crops had to be picked quickly, as soon as they were ready to avoid deterioration and to maximise value.

From the middle of the seventeenth century there was clearly insufficient local labour to cope with harvesting the hops so "strangers came a hopping". Hop growers attracted labour principally from the industrial areas of London, Birmingham and South Wales; therefore counties within easy reach of these places became the largest hop producers.

It became a condition of employment that the hoppers had to stay for three to four weeks until picking was complete, but fuel and shelter was provided. The quality of shelter varied from use of existing buildings, such as barns, lofts, stables and pigsties, to sheets of canvas slung across suitable supports; and from tents to tin and brick-built huts. As well as washing and toilet facilities, some sort of temporary or permanent cookhouse was also provided where meals could be prepared once the day's work was over.

Conditions improved greatly following the First World War, partly due to Public Health Inspectors, and hoppers came to regard picking as a month's paid holiday. However; from the 1950s, hoppers were finding better jobs with paid holidays. Driven by a loss of labour, mechanisation arrived to completely replace handpicking by 1970, and so 300 years of hoppers' holidays came to an end.

As I live and metal detect in Kent, it is more difficult to find farms that haven't been involved in hop growing than ones which have, and many are still growing hops. The losses in the ground, however, vary greatly from farm to farm and the major factor seems to be whether the farm had hoppers' accommodation or not. Many of the smaller concerns used only local pickers, who would commute between their own homes and the farm, carrying with them just their daily needs. Losses in such places tend to be relatively modest, although they can still extend back centuries and be very worthwhile.

Where accommodation was provided it was clearly to cater for imported hopping families who would live, work, play, sleep and eat on the farm for a whole month each year. Not only would these pickers bring whatever goods and chattels they needed for their stay, but also store up their earnings for the return home. More time spent on the land with more artefacts multiplies the losses.

So, if you are interested in finding your share of hoppers' losses, there are three things you need to look for to maximise your chances of success,

Firstly, if you don't know already, I suggest you find out exactly where hops were grown in your locality, which you can discover from the Internet by doing a search on [county name] hops. If you do not have Internet access, similar information should be available from the research section of your local library. (I say "were" grown, as current growers will probably be reluctant to let you and your detector loose on their hop gardens because of the risk of spreading Verticillium Wilt, a particularly nasty plant disease that puts hop gardens out of action for a number of years.)

Secondly, look out for hop kilns, called oast houses in the South East, which still stand in many hop growing areas. Many of them have been converted into dwellings as modern industrial drying has made them obsolete for their original purpose. From the eighteenth century most hop farms had their own kilns consisting of brick-built circular towers with conical roofs, each topped by a wooden cowl that was usually painted white.

In the early twentieth century kiln design changed to square towers with pyramid roofs, which were easier to build and run. The 1930s saw changes in the drying process to fan assisted oil-fired hearths, which resulted in many of the cowls being replaced with louvered "boxes".

Thirdly, have a look at large-scale Ordnance Survey maps for evidence of pickers' huts, which are shown usually as long narrow constructions, often isolated from other farm buildings.

A former hop farm was actually the first farm I searched and it was only curiosity over why I was finding so many coins and artefacts that Eric, the farmer, shared with me his considerable knowledge of the farm's history. The farmhouse dated to 1475, but other than that there were no standing buildings of any historical significance. Or rather that is to say with the possible exception of the barn, which appeared to date back a couple of hundred years and seemed to have been built over an earlier structure. The farm mainly now grew fruit, but had grown hops for some considerable time until the third quarter of the twentieth century. This was evidenced by five blocks, or barracks, of pickers' huts that were shown on the 1908 Ordnance Survey map. The fields in which these huts stood were almost carpeted with coins, badges, buckles, buttons and jewellery dating from Georgian to recent times.

Moving out to the other fields away from the huts where the hops were formerly grown, losses contemporary with the hoppers thinned out; however, earlier finds appeared. I actually found my first Roman coin, my first hammered silver coin, and my first crotal bell here. Another first was the barrel and box of a Belgian gentleman's travelling pocket or lady's muff pistol dating late eighteenth century.

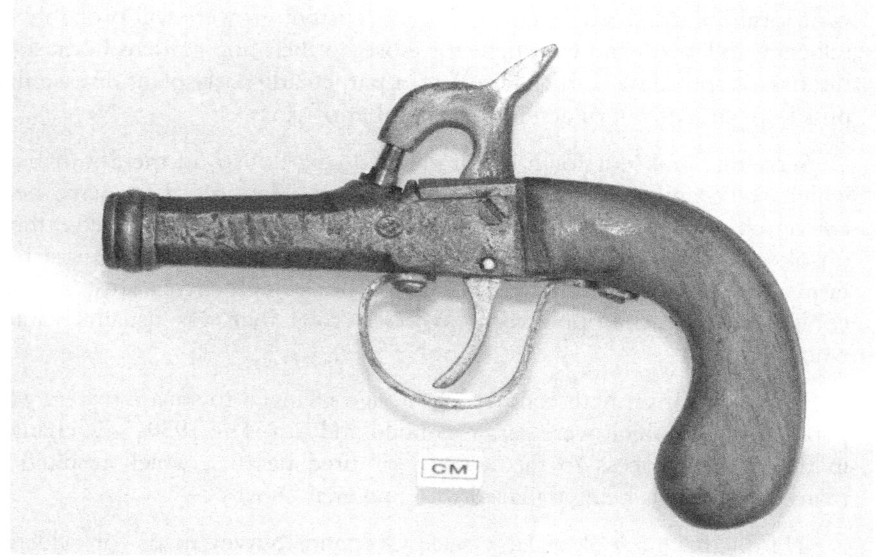

I have searched a number of farms since, which have been involved in hop growing. It is those that have evidence of pickers' huts, which always offer the best sport. It doesn't seem to matter how recent the huts appear to be, for the accommodation must have developed over the years and earlier tents, or use of farm buildings, would not show up on maps.

So, if you have access to suitable locations, give hop gardens a try and you could be filling your finds bag like never before.

Ploughing Matches. The agricultural community has a love for older engine and horse powered machinery and organise matches all around the Country to put these machines to the test against others in their class. There is a large gathering of farmers and landowners, who you may be able to approach for search permission, as well as the general public adding to losses already on the site of the match.

Rabbit Warrens. Rabbits or conies were introduced into Britain by the Normans for their meat and fur. Vast numbers of rabbits and hares were farmed by warreners in domestic warrens, often of immense size and complexity. A water-filled ditch or moat was usually provided to keep the rabbits from escaping, and a fence, was erected to keep out predators. The most characteristic structure of the warren is the pillow mound. These were oblong mounds with flat tops, often these had pre-built, stone-lined tunnels. The preferred location was on a gentle slope, to aid drainage. The soil needed to be soft, to accommodate further burrowing. Domestic warrens are now obsolete, but numerous pillow mounds and other remains can still to be found.

Medieval pillow mound at Stoke Poges. Photo: Bob Embleton, CC BY-SA 2.0, https://commons.wikimedia.org/w/index.php?curid=13449424

Windmills date back to the twelfth century in Britain. Owners of grain brought it to the corn mill where they had to pay the miller to turn the grain into flour, so there would be much coinage involved. Not all windmills ground grain but whatever they were used for the principle would be much the same. Looking at old 6 in to 1 mile, or larger, Ordnance Survey maps are a good way of spotting old sites. The National Library of Scotland has a massive collection of old ordnance survey maps online; you can overlay modern aerial maps on them too: https://maps.nls.uk/geo/explore. For the unconnected the local library is the place to go. Old folks may remember seeing windmills on high ground. Other clues may take the form of pub or road names, 'mill road' or 'mill cottage' for example. Footpaths leading to hilltops from several directions often converge at windmill site.

3 BUILDINGS

Buildings of any sort where you can gain access to the surrounding ground or even the interior of the building itself, will be worth searching. There will possibly be items to find from the land use before construction, disturbed ground during construction, the workforce involved in construction, the building's use and visitors. The older and wealthier the building, the greater the chance of outstanding finds.

Abandoned and Derelict Buildings and Land. There are a number of such properties scattered around the UK. The Bishops Avenue, Hampstead, North London, dubbed Millionaire's Row, actually contains 16 derelict luxury properties. Potters Manor House, Crowborough, Sussex, was deserted for years and is now owned by the actress, Cate Blanchett. Some 40 such properties are detailed at: https://www.atlasobscura.com/things-to-do/england/abandoned

If you come across an apparently abandoned property you first need to try and find the owner to seek search permission. Check with the nearest house, pub, post office, estate agents and if that draws a blank contact the local council or Land Registry. If you fail to find an owner and the property is without adverse signage and easily accessible you could investigate without a metal detector or tools in the first instance. If anyone challenges you, you may have located the owner to ask for permission. Do not get into an argument, apologise and leave, as necessary. If nobody objects you may consider returning with a metal detector but bear in mind that you could be accused of theft, if the owner turns up.

Although not definite proof, here are a few signs that may help identify abandoned property.

*Windows and doors boarded up.

*Gardens not maintained and overgrown.

*The property has been uninhabited for years and neighbours are unaware of anyone living there.

*The garden is used for fly tipping.

*The property needs considerable repair.

*There have been previous reports of squatters.

*Signs of vermin.

Bridges can date back to Roman times although most will be post medieval. Packhorse bridges generally date before 1800. Plenty of scope here. Traditionally people crossing water threw a coin in for safe crossing. Clearly it would be an important and well used crossing to warrant the expense of a bridge and considerable labour would be involved.

Cafes. Disused cafes are quite common, many failed when motorways were opened leaving the once busy main roads empty for a time. Some were demolished and others became houses.

Castles. To control his new kingdom, William I built castles, initially of the motte and bailey type, commanding strategic positions throughout the land. The function of a castle was both offensive and defensive; protecting the garrison, while enabling control of surrounding areas with raiding parties. Although essentially military, the structures also served as centres of administration and symbols of power, particularly as stone walls replaced wooden. Castles were used to control the local population, major travel routes, and features important to communal life, such as mills and fertile land. Castle building continued right through the medieval period but went into rapid decline soon afterwards, as cannon fire became powerful enough to penetrate stone walls.

A Castle itself could be an amazing detecting site, if you could gain legal access. As you would expect, many castles are scheduled and out of bounds. Nevertheless there are still opportunities; some castles are in private ownership and the owner may allow a search of the grounds, benefitting from some help with running costs and/or historical interest. In 1995 a large metal detecting rally took place in the grounds of Chilham castle, Kent, for instance. Much of the land surrounding castles has been sold off over the years and the current landowners may be more agreeable to giving search permission, than the castle owners. This proved fortuitous for me, when I gained permission for a field that had been divorced from a castle park, years ago, and turned out to be the site of a hundred meeting place. There is also the half-mile radius rule: search any land you can gain permission on, within half a mile of a castle and interesting finds are bound to turn up. Remember, the Middleham Jewel and Ring were found a short distance from Middleham Castle.

Castles are a popular topic and there is plenty of information online or available at your library. The lists of British castles online: https://en.wikipedia.org/wiki/Category:Lists_of_castles_in_the_United_Kingdom cover some 400 castles in depth.

Churches A feature of medieval Britain was the establishment or rebuilding of parish churches in stone. The Normans rebuilt many of the earlier Saxon churches, to standardise their appearance to the Norman model and church building continued apace until the Tudor era. There are some 8500 English medieval churches still standing, although many will have been much repaired and restored.

The origin of the English parish is uncertain but at least some parish boundaries may have been those of Saxon manors. The term: parish; originally referred to a bishop's administrative district but evolved to mean the area around a church. Since there are 12,600 ecclesiastical parishes in England, while Scotland and Wales have some 900 each, then at least that amount of churches must have been built.

The church was the centre of parish life and would have seen much coming and going resulting in losses in the ground from poor and wealthy alike. While grave plots are generally owned by relatives of the deceased and it would be unwise to detect them unless specifically requested by the owner, any open areas will repay searching. Pay attention to paths, gates, trees and inside and outside churchyard walls. Churches are always short of money and an offer to the vicar or rector to share the value of the finds or a suitable donation could secure permission. Try and include the vicarage or rectory as well, since countless church fetes would have been held there. Whatever its age, the church may have been built on a sacred site going back to prehistoric times, so any fields or open land around the church should also be on your radar, particularly those with footpaths leading to the church.

Colleges & Universities can date back hundreds of years, often have a lot of land (not necessarily just the campus) and may allow metal detecting, perhaps for a specific project or if you are a student of the establishment.

Converted Buildings. Many formerly busy buildings such as schools, rectories, and pubs have been sold off and converted into private dwellings, often with their former gardens or playgrounds largely intact. Look for Old School House, Red Lion Cottage, etc.

Dovecotes were built by the nobility in medieval times for rearing doves and pigeons for meat and eggs and are usually associated with castles and manor houses. The feathers were used for stuffing cushions and the dung as fertilizer. Not only are they an indicator of a wealthy property, they will have been regularly visited.

Dwellings Let's start at the beginning by finding things, eyes only and we'll start at home with some 'armchair' treasure hunting. The act of sitting tends to open up trouser pockets allowing coins and other objects to fall out and disappear down the gaps at the back and edges of armchairs and sofas. Remove all loose cushions, kneel on the seat facing the back, which depresses the seat cushion making it easier to slide your hand carefully (you could find sharp objects) down and along all gaps, retrieving whatever you find. Check under all furniture for lost objects by either moving the furniture or using a flashlight or torch. Check drawers, particularly 'junk' draws for misplaced money and objects. Look in all travel bags and suitcases. Check the pockets of all clothes and the floor of the wardrobe, closet or clothes cupboard. All properties have nooks and crannies that tend to collect money and misplaced items so have a good look around your own home and pick up any money and valuables. If you have an old house with floorboards, perhaps when you are changing a carpet, pull up any loose floorboards and look carefully beneath also run the hook of a wire clothes hanger in the gaps between the skirting boards and floor.

We can extend the search further to include deliberate hiding places for hoards of coins, banknotes or other valuables, for even today there are still many people who don't trust banks and even more trusting souls, tend to keep coins at home. Even if you and your family don't hide cash and valuables at home, there's no telling what former occupiers may have done and old coins can be worth far more than their face value. I have found coins pushed in gaps in cladding on an old staircase newel post. Sometimes such posts are fitted with hollow knobs and banister railings may have hollow spokes. Children were fond of pushing coins into the keyhole of large old door locks, where they fell into the bottom. These locks are quite easy to dismantle to remove the coins. The fireplace deserves particular attention; many coins and hoards have been found hidden up the chimney, behind loose bricks, under loose flagstones in the hearth and behind the mantelpiece.

One place to check is the attic, not only may there be old forgotten 'junk' up there which may not be junk today but roof spaces are common hiding places for hoards. Check under any flooring. Check along the joists and rafters for any packet or container fixed to them. A popular hiding method is to use a magnet as a retainer or magnetic key box attached to metal joining plates. A compass will come in handy for looking for these as the needle will swing to the magnetized area when you get close to it.

Search along the eaves if they are reasonably accessible and look beneath any insulation appearing disturbed.

The cellar is another area deserving a thorough search. Dark corners, exposed piping, wiring and ceiling joists are excellent hiding places. Check dirt floors for any signs of digging and run your metal detector over it. Patches in cement floors have yielded many a hoard. Check also any tunnels leading off the cellar for signs of disturbance. Sometimes pipes and conduit going nowhere will have valuables inside and false water taps which easily unscrew are not uncommon.

All outbuildings should be inspected similarly to attics and cellars. Greenhouses may have extra hiding places in pots and seed trays. And finally the garden, where a metal detector, can be most usefully employed to search all open space. Pay particular attention to the areas around the main doors into the property as transactions with tradesmen would have taken place here in the past. Hoards are often found under doorsteps, particular the rear step out of sight of prying eyes and also under paving stones. Washing put out to dry often had coins left in pockets, which fell to the ground during drying. People are attracted to trees for sitting or picnicking under or as a marker for a buried hoard. An old property may have a dump, formerly for household rubbish, but now rich in antiques. Objects were accidently or even deliberately dropped into wells. Never descend into a well without being tethered to the top by a strong rope, with a responsible person keeping a watchful eye on you from above. Bear in mind also that a well is a confined space and you could suffocate through noxious gasses or lack of oxygen; ideally check the atmosphere with a gas detector first and at the hint of breathing difficulties get out!

Now you know how to search a house you may want to find other properties on which to practice your new found skills. You probably have friends, relatives and neighbours who may be willing to let you go over their homes for a share of the proceeds or even just the experience. It used to be fairly easy to get permission to search properties due for, or undergoing, demolition by coming to some arrangement with the site manager; these days with health and safety concerns and greater appreciation of what might be found it is almost a closed door unless you are in the building or demolition trade. If you are involved in a house clearance at anytime you may be able to put your skills to work then. I know my late father was fond of hiding banknotes under the corner of the living room carpet and when my grandmother died the family found her mattress stuffed with banknotes, just before it ended up on the bonfire!

While people moving home and owners of an old property may be willing to let you search their house or grounds and valuable items may turn up, research can find properties which are much more likely to reward the search well. Keep it local, you don't want to be spending time and money travelling afar, when there will be plenty to look for on your doorstep. Old council records, local newspapers, almanacs, other local histories and talking to senior citizens will help you discover properties where hoards have been hidden and not recovered. Wealthy individuals who died suddenly, recluses, criminals may all have hidden hoards. Garden finds of old or ancient coins or artefacts may reveal more to a metal detector search of the grounds. Approach the current occupier with your research and you will probably win permission for a search. Offer a 50/50 split on the proceeds and try to obtain a signed written agreement.

Follies. The aristocracy and nouveau riche of the eighteenth century had a passion for creating false ruins and ornamental buildings of no practical purpose. These were on wealthy estates and will have been a magnet for the household and visitors alike. There were also military follies built to repel invaders that did not materialise.

Garages and Service Stations. From the humble lock-up to large service station, all attract people and would be worth searching outside and inside, wherever you can gain permission.

Hotels, Motels, Guest Houses, Holiday Homes Moving on to hotel rooms or even holiday homes in which you are staying, many travellers hide valuables during their stay, which are often forgotten when they leave. Reasons for hiding include fear of losing valuables, being robbed and reserving funds for fuel and food to get home. Bear in mind valuable items must be returned if you can identify the owner, who could have stayed at anytime in the past. Anything crime related such as drugs or firearms should be left alone and reported to management and police.

When searching the room or property do not damage anything; you can be sure no one will hide things in inaccessible places and if you cause damage the only thing you will gain is an extra bill at the end of your stay. You will find a torch or flashlight a useful item to include in your luggage.

Firstly, sit down and look around, identify places that are not cleaned regularly such as the tops of tall furniture as well as the backs, if the furniture is freestanding. Look behind any furniture that is against a wall. Look under the bed, right under the mattress and examine any removable bed posts. Check around the edge of the carpet for any places where banknotes could be slid under. Check chairs for any slits where banknotes could be hidden.

Check all draws and pull out any removable draws to check for anything taped to the backs or bottoms. Check the bottom of the unit with the draws out. Thumb through the pages of all books, magazines and brochures for banknotes and check spines for any spaces between the cover and binding where a note or two could be slipped. Check lamp bases, hollow stems, bulb holders and the inside of opaque shades for items that might be taped there.

Similarly examine underneath flowerpots and those with removable plastic flowers may have valuables hidden under the arrangement. Check any hollow tubing such as in furniture, hanging rails and shower rails for rolled up banknotes. Check clocks, radios, televisions and telephones for items slid or taped under the unit or inside any accessible compartments.

In the bathroom look under the sink and vanity tops carefully but beware of old razor blades and needles. Remove the top of the cistern, check under the lid inside the cistern and between the cistern and the wall.

You may be able to get permission to search the grounds with a metal detector, particularly with smaller establishments. Pay particular attention to areas that seem well-used such as outdoor seating and smoking areas.

Ice houses were built and used on prosperous British estates from around 1660 until superseded by refrigerators in the early twentieth century. Various types and designs of ice house exist but were commonly brick-lined, domed structures, with most of their volume sunk in, or covered by, earth. Ice houses varied in design but usually had conical or round bottoms to hold ice and allow the melt-water to drain away. Ice houses, also called ice wells, ice pits, or ice mounds can be found on contemporary maps. During the winter, the ice house was packed with ice and snow harvested from lakes or rivers, mixed with, usually straw, insulation. The ice would stay frozen for months, often until the following winter. The main application was the storage of perishable foods, but it could also ice drinks or make ice cream and frozen desserts. Searching around the ice house and the paths leading to it should produce finds. The drain system may also be profitably searched, perhaps from the outside. If the ice house is intact, it could hold poisonous and explosive gases; only venture inside using confined space entry approved safety procedures.

Inns, Pubs, and Taverns were the forerunners of today's hotel and can date back for centuries. It was the Romans who brought wine shops, known as *tabernae,* to Britain as well as the *mansio* or stopping place often built near springs. Such establishments were quickly built alongside Roman roads and in towns to help quench the thirst of the legions and accommodate officials. Ale, without hops, was the native British brew, and it appears that alehouses developed from taverns to provide the locals with their favourite drink. The Romans are also supposed to have introduced games like draughts and noughts and crosses. Inns survived and continued to adapt to a changing clientele through Saxons, Vikings, and Normans. Taverns sold wine to the richer clientele and along with alehouses provided food and drink, whilst inns offered accommodation for travellers, rich and poor. Alehouses, inns, and taverns collectively became known as public houses in the seventeenth century.

Early inns were established by religious houses and are often found close to churches. By the fifteenth century, inns and public houses were established along major highways at crossroads and ferries.

A 1577 survey counted 17,000 alehouses, 2,000 inns and 400 taverns throughout England and Wales. At this time travellers generally rode on horseback and inns hired out fresh horses which had to be kept close by. Fields or any open land around such inns will be well worth searching.

The coaching age, following the English Civil War, heralded another new era for the pubs of the time, as coaching inns were established on strategic routes around the country. Such inns provided food, drink and accommodation for passengers and crew alike, as well as fresh horses for their continued journey. You can recognise a coaching inn by its large arch into a courtyard or coach house. A typical coaching inn may have had as many as 60 people staying every night of the week with substantial sums of money in a confined space and its owners often under the influence of alcohol. Gambling was rife in the eighteenth century and much wagering took place around roadside inns. Cockfighting, dog fights, and boxing matches were typical and attracted large crowds of punters. In the nineteenth century, many pubs offered outdoor entertainment in the form of bowling, quoits, and the like which will also generate losses. You can find many of these pubs in Victorian local histories, guide books, street directories, and old Ordnance Survey Maps.

You are unlikely to be able to search inside an operating pub but the gardens and grounds offer plenty of scope. Thousands of these establishments have closed, many being converted into private houses, which will be worth tracking down from old maps and guides.

More pubs than you might expect have gardens and during the summer months, they can be packed. These sites resemble parks, but generally speaking finds (and ring-pulls) are more concentrated.

If you are a regular of the pub then getting permission to search the garden during the bleak winter months should be easy.

NOTE: Several hoards have been found near pubs.

<u>Inn Signs.</u> Publicans were compelled by law to display a sign from the fourteenth century. Large colourful signs were erected to attract travellers

from a distance. Signs often gave information on history: *The Centurion, Flowering Spring, Chequers, Ivy leaf, Bunch of Grapes, Bush, Noughts and Crosses,* may indicate Roman origin or nearby site. *The Roman Galley* in Kent was named after a nearby Roman shipwreck. *The Anglo-Saxon, Alfred the Great, King Harold, Battle of Hastings, William the Conqueror, The Curfew*, indicate medieval association. There is a *King Ethelbert* next door to a Saxon church at Reculver, Kent. Names based on twelfth century supply of alcohol and revelry to crusaders are: *The Bleeding Heart, Heart in Hand, The King, Coeur de Leon, Saracen's Head, Turk's Head, Lamb and Flag, Trip to Jerusalem*; on feudalism: *The Castle, Tything Man, Lord of the Manor;* on Pilgrimages and religion: *Weary Friar, Church House, Pilgrims, Adam and Eve, Cross Keys, Three Fishes* and on paganism: *Maypole, Jack in the Green.* Other names were based on entertainment, clientele or topographical information: *The Cock* (cock fighting), *The Bear* (bear baiting), *Thatchers Arms, Miners Arms, Miners Standard, Pig of Lead, Packhorse Inn, The Drovers, Running Pump* (a watering place), *Salters Gate* (transporters of salt), *Five Ways* (crossroads), *Stepping Stones* (river crossing), *Volunteer*, (rifle range nearby), *Boxers* (organised fights), *Beacon* (close to a beacon fire), *Chequers* (where moneylenders carried on business), *The Boot* (highwaymen) and *Tollgate* or *Tollbar* (where tolls were collected).

Manor Houses. Associated with the church in medieval Britain was the manor. In fact, traditionally the lord of the manor built the estate church before the Church itself became wealthy enough to fund its own building; thus older manor houses usually have a church nearby. In England, southern Scotland and some Welsh lowlands farming was organised around the manor in a pattern known as open field farming. Under this system, the plough land consisted of between two and five enormous fields. Each field was divided into a large number of strips shared out amongst the community. The villagers cooperated with their neighbours to work their own land and the demesne lands of the lord of the manor, such that the entire field was put into the same crop (or left fallow). It was a complex system of which books have been written but the point is that (except for Kent and East Anglia) the strip farming left a characteristic ridge and furrow identification in permanent pasture, highlighting medieval manors.

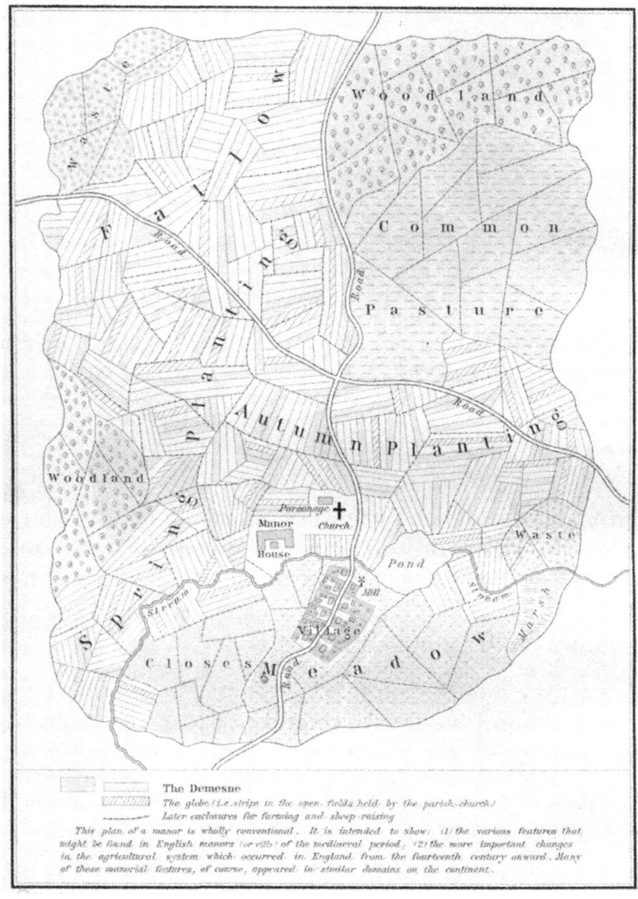

While you could swing your metal detector anywhere around one of these manorial sites, as you never can tell what you might find, you would be best concentrating on the vicinity of the manor and church, where the wealth was. The average peasant working in the fields would be lucky to have two cut farthings to rub together, whereas the rich lord of the manor could abseil down his mountain of cash.

I took part in a club search of the grounds of a medieval manor house, with a generous garden of about nine acres. Although eighteen of us only searched for four hours, we found well over fifty coins and artefacts, several of which were silver. In addition, I made one gold find here, a Tudor iconographic finger ring. The ring was declared treasure and remains my most valuable single find to date.

The grounds of standing manor houses would be excellent for searching but there are also thousands of former manor houses and associated parks, throughout the country, which have disappeared, and are now accessible farmland. There is an Internet site, which boasts a complete list of lost English country houses numbering 1999:

http://www.lostheritage.org.uk/lh_complete_list.html However, while the site has an impressive list, I can add five lost manor houses within ten miles of my home.

So how does something as large as a manor house become lost? One of the main reasons seems to be destruction by fire; another is the family outgrew the house and rebuilt nearby. Often the house was surplus to requirements, the family having gained other houses by marriage or inheritance. Whatever the reason for the house being abandoned, the buildings often disappeared because valuable building materials were taken for reuse elsewhere.

While the manor house may have disappeared, often it is remembered in a remaining feature or a name, such as: fishponds, dovecote, moat, ice house, gatehouse, lodge, chapel or park. It is common for the manor name to have been given to a standing building or wood or recorded as a field name on a tithe map. If a manor house was destroyed by fire, the name Burnt House is a reliable clue to the event.

Monastery Sites The Normans embarked on a massive program of religious building. According to some historians, it was to appease God for killing the English in battle. In 1066, religious houses in England and Wales, including colleges and hospitals, numbered below 300. By the end of the twelfth century the total had risen to over 1300, owing mainly to the establishment of monastic houses. The military orders, Knights Templars and Knights Hospitallers, were founded along with many hospitals. The number of religious houses continued to rise to over 2000 in the mid-fourteenth century but dropped below 1700 in the following one hundred years mainly because of the severe reduction in population following the Black Death of 1348-9.

The 1534 Act of Supremacy made Henry VIII the Supreme Head of the Church of England, divorcing England from the Pope's authority. This and following acts gave the King the authority to dissolve monasteries in England, Wales and Ireland, and confiscate their income and assets. This dissolution of the monasteries, occurred between 1536 and 1540, and affected all monasteries and related parts, including abbeys, priories, convents, nunneries, hospitals, colleges and friaries. Only a few religious houses in England and Wales survived by special dispensation or were converted into parochial use, while in Ireland, where Henry had less control and profit, a considerable number survived into the next century. Independent Scotland abolished the papacy in 1560 and James VI confiscated the estates of bishops and monasteries under The Act of Annexation in 1587.

Confiscated silver and gold plate was minted into coins, while the lead stripped from roofs was sold to swell the royal coffers. Buildings and land passed initially to the Crown then the majority fell into the hands of nobles and gentry by royal gift or purchase. A few buildings survived more or less intact but, without roofs, most became ruinous and quarries for building material.

Since the main reason for the plunder was financial gain, it follows that the majority of religious houses were rich and some of those riches, as lost or hidden coins and artefacts, are lying around nearby waiting for a metal detector to pass over them, providing we can gain permission. Like castles, many sites will be scheduled and out of bounds but others are in private hands and more have disappeared without trace. Religious Houses are another popular topic with considerable information online and in libraries. It is perhaps worth pointing out that The National Archives is the repository for State records, and while delving into their documents can be heavy going, particularly in the medieval period, they produce many user friendly guides (online and in print) on a wide range of topics which may direct you to secondary sources (e.g. modern books) as well as their primary sources. The monastic guide is here:

http://www.nationalarchives.gov.uk/help-with-your-research/research-guides/religious-houses-lands-1000-1530/

Public Conveniences are clearly built where they would be used so searching around them should turn up losses from those 'spending a penny'. Many have been closed but can be found from old guides.

Schools in the UK date back to the sixth century and were largely linked to religious establishments until the nineteenth century, although charity schools and Free Grammar Schools had developed since late medieval times. A string of legislation from 1870 brought compulsory and eventually free education and a rapid expansion in the number of schools. Clearly schools were attended by large numbers of pupils and teachers on a daily basis, holidays excepted, with great opportunity for metallic losses in the grounds. It may be difficult to gain access to schools still functioning but there are many that have closed down and permission to search their former grounds may now be obtained. Check old maps for former school sites.

Towers. Simple towers like lighthouses, bell towers, clock towers, signal towers, minarets and watch towers were used to communicate information over greater distances. While not usually occupied as such, all were manned to a greater or lesser extent and were landmarks.

Tunnels. There are several groups of tunnels that would be worthwhile detecting. Probably the most numerous and potentially profitable, are those associated with religious houses such as abbeys, hospices, monasteries and priories. Most of the tunnels were part of a fresh water feed and effluent system, which have seldom been investigated and may hold treasures secreted there during the Dissolution. The discharge point into river or soak-away, would be worth finding and may be well away from the buildings and scheduling.

*Smugglers tunnels, usually coastal, were used to hide and move contraband. Research into local smuggling activity may find them.

*Castles often had defensive tunnels or sally ports permitting stealthy exits and entrances. These could exit a considerable distance from the castle.

*Manor houses and even palaces sometimes had tunnels built for various reasons such as pleasure, political subterfuge, privacy and security.

*Sewage systems, particularly ancient systems under large cities, especially London. Original outfalls would be worth finding and searching around.

*Tunnels were created by eighteenth century aristocrats as follies or hideaways for quasi-religious cults and hellraisers.

*Tunnels were used during WWII for defence and hideouts. Rail mounted guns were kept in railway tunnels, the railway may now be disused.

Windmills were introduced into Europe a thousand years after watermills. The horizontal-axis or vertical (sail) windmill, was first used in north-western Europe in the twelfth century. The post mill is the earliest European flour mill, where the mill's body pivots on a large vertical post to catch the wind for economical operation in variable wind direction. The first post mills had the post sunk into an earth mound for support. Later, a wooden tripod was developed, often covered for weather protection and to provide storage space. In the late thirteenth century, taller masonry tower mills were built, on which only the cap rotates, fitted with longer sails which can work in low winds.

The smock mill developed from the tower mill, where a board or similar covered wooden framework replaced the tower. Smock mills originated for pumping water for drainage, where their light weight made them less prone to sink in marshy areas. They were also popular owing to cheaper construction and used for grinding grain, fulling cloth, sawing, papermaking and latterly electricity generation.

Post mills were the most numerous in Europe until overtaken by smock and tower mills in the nineteenth century. The sites of windmills, whether existing, derelict of vanished are excellent for metal detecting. A long line of visitors would have paid the miller for his services and lost metal objects in the process.

4 CONSTRUCTION AND DEMOLITION

Construction and demolition sites are well-worth searching as much is exposed that would normally be out of reach of your detector. A few years ago you could walk onto such a site, have a chat to the person in charge and readily get permission to detect there. Unfortunately, mainly owing to health and safety issues, you will be hard pressed to even enter such a site. If you happen to work in the construction industry, then you are much better placed to gain permission to search construction sites. Other than that, you may gain permission on small projects and especially those, where you know someone working there, know the landowner, or if you can make friends with JCB drivers, builder's labourers, trench diggers, or drain layers.

There is another way and that is to keep an eye on the planning register and get involved early. Planning applications cover all sorts of property and projects from a modest householder building a garage through lords building staff accommodation and farmers erecting new buildings, to major housing or industrial developments. Some planning applications, such as demolition, tree surgery and sign erection do not involve construction. Also the planning application may fail or be withdrawn and even construction projects may have considerable areas of land outside the actual building works where permission to detect may be forthcoming. So keeping an eye on planning applications is a worthwhile pursuit if only to build up a database of landowners for possible future use.

Planning is the responsibility of local authorities who must make the details of all planning applications available to the public. This is principally to allow anyone to object or comment on the content. The procedure does vary slightly around the country; however the information will be available and accessible. As usual it is always best to start with an area that you know.

If you know the name of the local authority you can look them up in the telephone directory (local libraries keep a wide range of directories) or type name + planning in an Internet search engine. If you don't know who the local authority is, there is a search facility on the Planning Portal website: http://www.planningportal.gov.uk or you can ask directory enquiries for the town hall or council offices, which will then put you in touch with planning.

All planning authorities must publish a Planning Register and are legally obliged to make this available to the public. Applications are normally published weekly, however the register goes back to 1974 so if you spot a fairly recent structure on land that interests you, you can often get the landowner's details from the associated application months or years previously. You can consult this register at the planning department office and it may be available elsewhere: council offices, libraries and certainly on the Internet. While the Internet is the most convenient for computer users, the amount of information available may be limited. Even so you should be able to obtain the applicant's name and address for recent applications although this will not necessarily be the landowner as sometimes an agent is used whose name and address is given. You could still contact the landowner for search permission by sending a letter via the agent or find the landowner from the Land Registry. If you need more information than is available on the Internet you will have to visit the planning department office, where you will normally find the staff very helpful, owing to their legal obligation to the public.

Typically the Planning Register will contain the following information:

Application number:

Application type:

Registration Date:

Comments welcome by:

Committee date:

Location: (address of property)

Ward:

Proposal: (the intended work)

Case Officer: (for council)

Case Officer Tel:

Status:

Registered Agent:

Applicant: (property owner or agent (if name and address is same as registered agent))

Decision:

Appeal Received Date:

In addition there will be other associated documentation, sometimes available on-line, e.g.

Application Form

Associated Documents

Plans/Drawings

Site Plan

Archaeological survey reports

All projects breaking ground, will have some type of archaeological investigation prior to construction starting and you may be able to get involved at that stage. In Kent, for instance, KAMSU organises metal detectorists from clubs to take part in archaeological investigations.

When a Greenfield site is being developed the topsoil has to be removed and this is usually piled up on site in a large heap depending on space available. Often subsoil is being removed and that will be piled up separately. If soil is being taken off site, try and find out where it is being taken as you may still be able to search it.

When you arrive at the site, if building has yet to start, you should have a level stretch of land to search. Systematically search every inch of ground, investigating every signal, however faint.

It may take several days to make a thorough search, but when you are sure there is nothing else left to find, try the topsoil and subsoil spoil heaps. Although they will be high it should be relatively easy to reach the top as usually at one end there will be a gentle slope to facilitate earthmovers climbing the mound. After you have searched the top sweep your detector over the edge on the sides of the heap as far as you can reach, without toppling over the edge. Then return to the base of the heap and use the detector on the bottom few feet of the sides. There will probably be a large area around the sides you cannot reach with your metal detector. If the heap is relatively stable, it may be possible to climb up the sides and detect with care. A long-handled spade can be used as a support where necessary. As construction progresses some of the earth will be removed from the heap to be used as fill. This will expose unsearched spoil that was in the centre of the heap and will repay searching. If some interesting finds are made on the outer surface of a mound, it might be worthwhile, if possible, searching through the whole lot by systematically removing say a six inch layer at a time.

The final places on construction sites that must be worth searching are the excavations, with great care! Trenches are dangerous, unpredictable and confined spaces; there is risk of the sides collapsing, falling objects and becoming trapped. Never work alone. Deep excavations (over 1200mm) should have shuttering installed and are unlikely to be searchable with a metal detector. Search the bottom and sides of shallow trenches from within; do not stand on the edge of a trench and reach in with your detector, the sides could collapse under you. If you approach searching trenches sensibly you should keep safe and make some great finds.

I became very interested when I was told that a pipeline was being planned locally, accompanied by an archaeological survey covering a five metre wide swathe through around two-and-a-half miles of countryside. The reason I got to hear about the project was that it would cut across several farms upon which I already had search permission. The route of the pipeline was subject to much discussion over a couple of years, while landowners, environmentalists, planners and contractors deliberated over the ideal route. Eventually a course was determined with minimal interference to dormice, badgers and landowners' property, in that order.

With the first sod about to be cut I contacted the archaeologist in charge and offered my detecting expertise, which was graciously accepted. I was told that I would need to wear steel toe-capped boots, high visibility vest and a hard hat, which I was required to supply myself. Although I had the safety equipment left over from my former day job, this was a little new to me as on other archaeological digs I had been free to wear what I pleased. The difference here though was that mechanical excavators and other heavy plant were being employed from the start: whereas all previous digs had been surveys prior to plant being brought onto site. I turned up on site with my gear and was told to report to the site office for an induction. The site agent outlined the facilities and general rules, pointing out that I could be fined £5,000 or imprisoned for six months if I happened to kill a dormouse! He then went over the health and safety issues, which weren't too arduous and I was pleased to learn that wearing the hard hat was only compulsory when working around operating plant but not so pleased that my high visibility vest lacked the regulation number of reflective stripes: I had to go and buy a new one. I bought a new hard hat too as although the site agent didn't notice, my old hat was out of date so may not have given the required protection should I be unlucky enough to be hit on the head by a flying house-brick or similar.

On site, the first problem I had to overcome was detecting while wearing steel toe-caps. I figured that extending the detector stem to its maximum length would keep the search coil far enough in front of me to avoid false signals from my boots and happily this worked well. I always use a pair of headphones when detecting, which reduces background noise and allows me to hear fainter signals. The relaxed hard hat rule on this project rarely caused a problem with wearing headphones but a later project, where hard hats were compulsory at all times, was a real pain in that respect. I tried the headphones over the hat and the headphones fell off; I tried the headphones under the hat and the hat fell off. Eventually I found that, being good quality headphones with a volume control, I could just hang them around my neck at full volume and hear signals perfectly well.

As the finds were going to be stored and eventually returned to the relevant landowner, I was asked to bag all finds, other than obvious junk and hand them in to the archaeologists at the end of the day. After a few days and a few interesting finds had been made 1 was allowed to take the finds home overnight for minimal washing and photographing, so I was able to make a near complete photographic record of the metallic finds I made on this project. When I joined, there were two other friendly detectorists already engaged on the project, having previously worked with the archaeological contractors elsewhere. We tended to be assigned different sections to work so while we met up on occasion, we didn't usually work together.

My first few searches were on relatively flat ground but it wasn't long before the earth started piling up as first the topsoil and then the subsoil was removed from the easement, as the stripped area was called. As the spoil heaps needed searching as well as the exposed levels, the search method I adopted on the heap was to start at the top and work down as I figured I would catch any objects slipping downwards that I had dislodged with my feet. I did find a long handled spade to be very useful for support on the few occasions I slipped. Going along the top was fairly easy as was ground level, both being basically flat surfaces. Walking along half way up the side, trying to keep a foot-hold on a roughly forty-five degree angle of loose soil was something else! Nevertheless I came away from the completed project unscathed.

Land stripped of soil for pipe-laying

The first stretch of pipeline was laid along the road and no detecting was needed, which was just as well as I did not possess a long sleeved high visibility jacket, which is compulsory wear when working on public highways. I had never previously swung a detector on the first section through farmland so I was a little disappointed that the only finds of note were a couple of Venetian soldini or galley halfpennies. The archaeology was fairly poor too, with just one medieval building coming to light, which the archaeologists referred to as a hovel.

I was expecting much more of the next section, which I had been searching for years and had an apparent Saxon history, although I had made no finds of that period here. Despite there being plenty of metal in this field, previous good finds had been fairly scarce, about the best being half of a medieval mirror case. I suppose it wasn't too much of a surprise that I did not find much this time either: just a complete medieval buckle and a fourth century Roman bronze coin. The archaeologists only found a small amount of Bronze Age pottery, concluding that the archaeology had been largely obliterated by intensive farming.

The following section, area 10, ran through two fields that, again, had not received my attention previously. The second field did, however, run alongside an ancient track way, which had seen traffic for a couple of thousands of years and it was here that I found a King John penny on the surface of the spoil heap. That was, however, my only noteworthy find from this section before we were on to area 11, which I was familiar with, having gained search permission in the recent past.

Despite its promising pedigree, having the ancient track way on one side of the two fields and a once navigable river on the other, finds had been rather meagre but with the topsoil removed a few interesting finds emerged. In the first field where the easement ran alongside the track way, I found a Henry I penny, Edward III farthing, and a medieval pendant hanger. The archaeologists also uncovered a small Roman building here and an early-Roman bronze coin within the structure.

In the second field the easement cut sharply away from the track way and the only early find to emerge was a medieval casket key. I was however also pleased to find a seventeenth century token, which although in very poor condition was decipherable as being from The Chequers Inn, nearby.

Areas 12 to 17 belonged to a different landowner who had given me search permission many years ago. The land was apparently infested with dormice, for the contractors were ordered to construct a dormouse bridge across the easement at every point they breached a hedge and even when they went through existing gates. According to the environmentalists, dormice are incapable of travelling across the ground so had to have a bridge constructed for high-level travel. I did wonder how they managed when the farm gates were left open for weeks on end during harvest to facilitate machinery movement. I would have expected to have seen a queue of these tiny rodents at the gate post waiting patiently for somebody to come along and shut the gate! Then again I had not seen a single dormouse in the 15 or more years spent around this farm and even the farmer, who had lived here man and boy, only knew someone who had seen one!

Excavation on the first field was brought to an abrupt halt, not by dormice but by a family of badgers who had made their home right in the middle of the easement. As badgers are also a protected species the contractors had to apply for an eviction order or badger licence, which took three months to materialise. So, on to area 13, which although also running alongside an ancient track way had only ever yielded good finds on high days and holidays. It wasn't any better despite the excavation for I recorded precisely nothing of any age from here and neither did the archaeologists.

I was really looking forward to searching area 14 as it had often produced good finds from all periods in the past. I wasn't to be disappointed for among the many finds from this section were a crotal bell, spur buckle, Nuremberg jetton, pot leg, Roman coins, Thurrock type potin and a medieval strap end.

The archaeologists had a bit of excitement here too. Firstly a burial, which turned out to be a lamb and then the excavator driver spotted pottery, which was no mean feat from where he was sitting. Careful excavation revealed the pottery to be a Roman lantern, quite a find!

Area 15 had always been difficult to work because a Second World War Hurricane aeroplane had crashed here, exploding on impact and littering much of the field with small pieces of aluminium. I must have cleared most of the debris for I found little during the excavation. What did turn up though were some strange pieces of ironwork that looked like footplates on the old roller skates we used to strap onto our shoes in my youth; eventually they were identified as hippo sandals or Roman horseshoes.

I found a number of Roman coins covering the first to fourth centuries together with a few medieval pieces including a scabbard chape, a penny and short cross cut farthing. At around a metre below the original surface the archaeologists uncovered stonework which they thought was Roman and a non-ferrous signal I received in amongst the stones resulted in a heavy bronze "bead", which is probably a knife pommel.

Area 16, which had produced numerous Roman and medieval finds in the past turned out to be the archaeological jewel in the crown. Once the topsoil had been removed it was difficult to find somewhere to stand without treading on medieval archaeology. There was a baker's oven, a granary, medieval buildings and track ways, all in all forming a bakery complex serving a number of nearby watermills. I did well with the detector too, finding a short cross cut halfpenny, several Roman coins, again first to fourth centuries, a gilded medieval strap end with floral pattern, a medieval English jetton, a medieval ring brooch and an Iron Age brooch fragment.

Section 17 is one that you would expect great finds from. It is sandwiched between an ancient track way and a river; it boasts earthworks and Roman burials; it is adjacent to a medieval bakery and a hoard of Roman coins was found there. But if I searched the field all day I would be lucky to make one pre-Victorian find. I even organised a club rally here and we didn't make one good find each! I wondered if the pipeline excavation would make a difference: it did not. One fourth century Roman bronze coin was the sum total and no archaeology either. People in the past must have simply avoided this field.

There was only one field left now, the one with the badgers, who had left of their own accord by the time the licence came through: I expect they tired of the noise and fumes of the excavator as it frequently trundled past their abode. This has always been an interesting field, with the odd good find turning up from most periods of history so I was quite pleased to find a short cross cut halfpenny, three buckles from medieval times and a Tudor hook fastener.

But this field liked to keep its best until last, for just before the archaeologists signed off on this section, out popped a copper-alloy Iron Age strap junction of a form that the Museum of London describes as being probably used on a pony girth strap.

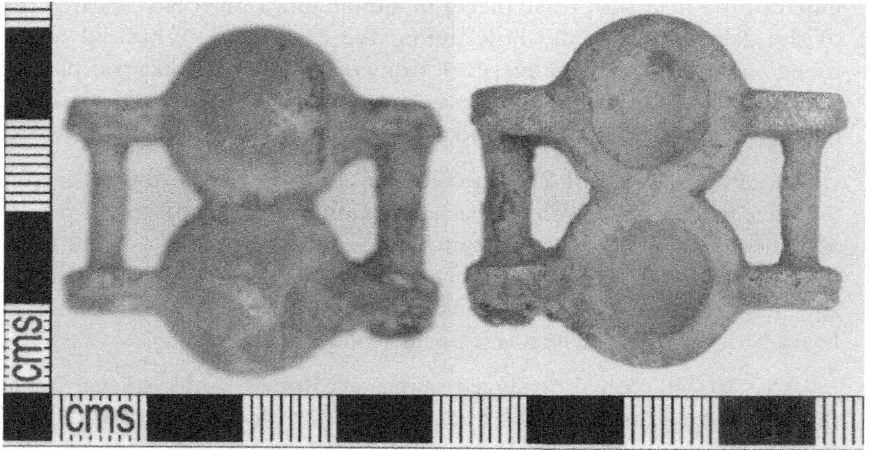

Iron-Age strap junction

5 CRIME AND PUNISHMENT

Criminal activities, such as robbery, can offer lots of good metal detecting locations, but clearly the whereabouts of hidden loot will be unknown. You will need to carry out research into local history, old newspapers and legends to pin-point likely locations and unearth their treasures.

Ducking stools were a women's punishment for the crimes of witchcraft, prostitution or simply being a scold. The ducking stool was a chair, slung over a river or pond, on a pivoted arm which allowed the victim strapped to the chair to be lowered and raised in and out of the water. The duration of the punishment could be brief or prolonged according to the sentence passed. As with any public punishment it attracted many spectators.

Footpads were robbers who travelled and stole on foot mainly from pedestrians or from transport left outside inns. They would frequent town streets and minor roads, often as part of a gang.

Gallows. Although originally for weighing large items, gallows were popularly used for execution from late medieval times. Permanent Gallows to act as a deterrent were erected, on a prominent hill outside city walls, or near the castle or other place of justice. Executions, especially of the notorious, attracted large crowds of spectators who undoubtedly dropped metal objects.

Gibbets. Gibbeting or hanging in chains was a punishment, which could be imposed as a means of or, more usually, in addition to execution. This practice started in medieval times as a deterrent to would be wrongdoers and was so widely used that in the Sixteenth century there were some 70,000 gibbets about the British countryside. The Murder Act 1751 empowered judges to impose gibbeting for murder and it was most often used for highwaymen, murderers, pirates, sheep stealers and traitors. The practice ceased in England in 1834. Gibbets were often placed alongside public highways (frequently at crossroads), waterways and high places where they could be seen for miles around. It is not for us to question how our ancestors derived their pleasures but apparently gibbets were a great attraction and also chips of wood taken from them would, supposedly, cure ailments such as ague and toothache. Place name research, particularly on tithe maps will often pinpoint gallows field or gibbet hill and there are other less obvious names like Swamstey, Warter, Worgret and Dethick, which are clues to such sites

Ghost Stories were often engineered by those engaged in criminal activity to deter people from finding their stash. So if you hear a ghost story, pay close attention to what was going on in the area.

Pirates. "With the name of pirate is also associated ideas of rich plunder, caskets of buried jewels, chests of gold ingots, bags of outlandish coins, secreted in lonely, out of the way places, or buried about the wild shores of rivers, and unexplored sea coasts, near rocks and trees bearing mysterious marks, indicating where the treasure was hid. And as it is his invariable practice to secrete and bury his booty, and from the perilous life he leads, being often killed or captured, he can never re-visit the spot again; immense sums remain buried in those places, and are irrecoverably lost. Search is often made by persons who labour in anticipation of throwing up with their spade and pickaxe, gold bars, diamond crosses sparkling amongst the dirt, bags of golden doubloons, and chests, wedged close with moidores, ducats and pearls; but although great treasures lie hid in this way it seldom happens that any is so recovered." From: Charles Ellms, *The Pirates Own Book, or Authentic Narratives of The Lives, Exploits and Executions of The Most Celebrated Sea Robber's*, (Portland ME, 1856). The opportunities for pirate hoards in Britain from the golden age of piracy, 1650-1730 are limited; however there are some possibilities in the Caribbean and Americas, particularly in connection with Drake, Gibbs and Morgan. The greatest opportunity for sites in Britain and Europe lie with the Viking raids of the Dark Ages.

The withdrawal of the Roman legions in the early fifth century left Britain less well defended against invaders from Scotland and from the sea. Sea going bands of Angles, Jutes and Saxons, who had designs on plunder and rich agricultural lands, continually raided the South and East coasts as they had under the Romans. From about 450 they settled in small independent communities, supplied by sea from their homelands. The **Anglo-Saxon Chronicle** tells us the Jutes, led by brothers Hengist and Horsa, were invited to assist the native Britons repel the invading northern

Scots and Picts, in exchange for food, money and land. This arrangement worked well until the Jutes decided conquest was preferable to servitude and joined forces with the Picts and Scots against the Britons. The Jutes took the land of Kent, southern Hampshire and the Isle of Wight. Meanwhile the Angles and Saxons colonised the east and south coasts, spreading westwards and northwards until by 600 only Cornwall, Devon, Cumbria, Scotland and Wales remained of the old British or Celtic kingdoms.

The Angles, Saxons and Jutes were neighbours in their Germanic homeland with similar cultures and for simplicity I will call them all Anglo-Saxons. They probably understood the Roman Civilisation but fiercely rejected the model as unsuited to their agricultural communities and way of life. As the migrants advanced, they sacked and burned the old Roman towns and villas, massacring or enslaving the Britons. The Anglo-Saxons constructed simple buildings of timber and thatch in villages and small towns near centres of agriculture, at river crossings or sites suitable for ports. They adopted the Roman system of agriculture and Anglo-Saxon finds are often made on late Roman rural sites.

The most significant early Anglo-Saxon landscape feature was the re-introduction of the earth barrow for pagan burials, which replaced Roman Christian interments. Prehistoric barrows were reused and new barrows constructed in cemeteries, usually located close to a river, estuary or the sea. The elite were buried in barrows with grave goods, often within an elaborately constructed chamber or a complete boat, such as that discovered at Sutton Hoo beside the River Deben in Suffolk. Tæppa's mound, another high-status barrow burial near the River Thames, is the origin of Taplow in Buckinghamshire.

Known barrows and cemeteries are normally scheduled and out of bounds to metal detecting but many have been ploughed-out and may be accessible, with permission. Those interred in barrows and cemeteries would have lived nearby and some cemeteries were dug out and the contents used to manure farmland in the eighteenth century. So you only need to search land around these barrows and cemeteries to find Anglo-Saxon coins and artefacts.

Following 150 years of pagan burials with potential grave goods, St Augustine arrived in 597 to convert Anglo-Saxons to Christianity eventually bringing an end to such practices. Change didn't happen overnight, it was a 'top down' conversion process starting with kings who welcomed recognition and support from the great Roman church. The kings passed their new religion down to their families and the aristocracy, while land, often on royal estates, was given to build Minster churches, which sent monks out into the surrounding communities to preach and convert the common people. Crosses were often erected to mark where preaching took place ahead of church building; a few stone crosses survive.

As an interesting approach to replacing paganism, churches were often built at pagan holy sites such as springs, wells and burial places. This displaced the old deities and commandeered some of the sanctity attributed by the common folk. So just search any fields around a church with Anglo-Saxon origins and you are likely to make finds from that period.

The policy of building churches on former holy sites continued well into medieval times so searching around old churches may turn up finds pre-dating the church.

By the end of the eighth century, the Anglo-Saxons had organised themselves by aggression or alliance into seven independent kingdoms. Meanwhile, the expanding Catholic Church had amassed significant amounts of gold and silver in coin and religious artefacts, which was mainly kept in the monasteries and minster churches. From 793, the Vikings, who were pagan Scandinavian pirates, from Denmark, Norway and Sweden, made hit-and-run raids against the British Isles. They targeted the undefended isolated monasteries for their rich pickings, particularly Lindisfarne, Wearmouth, Jarrow and Iona (Scotland). The Vikings attacked Scottish and Irish coastal districts in the first decade of the ninth century, southern England in 835 and the Welsh coast from the 850s.

From 865 the Vikings changed tack, seeing the British Isles' mild climate and fertile soil as a place for colonisation rather than plunder. Despite fierce resistance, Wales saw minor colonisation in coastal areas, while Scotland and the Irish coast were colonised relatively quickly compared to lowland Britain. All four countries of the British Isles have their own colourful history of the Viking invasions although I only have space to relate something of the fortunes of what became England.

The Great Heathen Army arrived in numerous ships, capturing York, which became the Viking capital. King Ethelred of Wessex, fought against the Vikings, until his death in 871, when he was succeeded by his younger brother, Alfred the Great. From 876 several Anglo-Saxon kings gave in to Viking demands for land, including Northumbria, Mercia and East Anglia. King Alfred continued to fight the invaders and defeated the Viking king, Guthrum of East Anglia at the Battle of Edington, Wiltshire. The Treaty of Wedmore, followed in 886, between East Anglia and Wessex, establishing a boundary between the Anglo-Saxons and the Viking area, called the *Danelaw*, since most Viking settlers were Danish.

Alfred formed a navy, organised a militia system and constructed a series of defended towns or *burhs,* providing secure refuges within a day's walk for the rural population. These *burhs,* some of which were re-fortified Roman towns, also served as regional market centres and mints. Wessex's modified defences were successful against renewed Viking attacks and in 896 the invaders dispersed, settling in East Anglia, Northumbria and Normandy. Opposition to Viking settlers continued under Alfred's successors. In 920 the Northumbrian and the Scots governments both submitted to the military power of Wessex. In 937 the Battle of Brunanburh, Cheshire, led to the collapse of Viking power in England and the eventual expulsion of the last Viking King of York, Erik Bloodaxe.

Under the reign of Edgar the Peaceful, England was politically unified and Edgar recognized as king of all England by both Anglo-Saxons and Vikings. Pagans were being converted to Christianity at home and abroad and there was a revival of the monasteries. However, during the reigns of his sons, Edward the Martyr, followed by Ethelred the Unready, the English monarchy declined in power and in 980 Viking raiders again attacked England. The English government decided that the way to stop these attacks was to pay the Vikings protection money and, in 991, they gave them £10,000 in *Danegeld.* This payment proved insufficient, and over the next decade the Vikings demanded increasingly larger sums of money. Many English called for hostile action to be taken against the Vikings, leading to Ethelred's 1002 cull, known as the St. Brice's Day massacre. The number killed is unknown but the event enraged the Vikings, precipitating more raids.

In 1013 King Sweyn of Denmark, who had previously made several attacks against England, invaded with a large army. Ethelred fled to Normandy, leaving Sweyn to take the English throne. Sweyn died within a year and Ethelred returned, but in 1016 another Viking army invaded, under the control of the Danish King Cnut. After defeating the Anglo-Saxons at the Battle of Assandun, Essex, Cnut became king of England as well as Denmark until his death in 1035, when England became independent again.

Edward the Confessor, Ethelred's son, reigned from 1042 and died in 1066, with neither heir nor a clear successor, but with three rival claimants to the throne. The king's council chose Harold of Wessex, Edward's brother-in-law, who was crowned Harold II. Later that year, Harald Hardrada, king of Norway, another claimant to the English throne, invaded Yorkshire and was defeated by Harold at the Battle of Stamford Bridge. Before the English Army had recovered, the Viking Normans, led by William the Conqueror, the third claimant to the throne of England, invaded from the south and triumphed at the Battle of Hastings. The Vikings won after all!

These were turbulent times that were bound to put losses in the ground for us to find. Various hoards of treasure were buried, some deposited by Anglo-Saxons attempting to hide their wealth from Viking raiders and others buried by Vikings to protect their loot. Whether it is hoards or casual losses you are looking for, you can increase your finds rate by doing your research and searching:

*As close as you can to places subjected to raids, such as monasteries.

*Battle sites. While known sites will probably be scheduled, the actual sites of battles in this period are mainly uncertain. You could set the record straight with your metal detector.

*Routes of marching armies; the Great Heathen Army travelled England for 14 years, which would have required many temporary camps. Vikings did not build temporary forts like the Romans so have left no clear trace in the landscape. However they did make camp for the winter in several places such as Thetford, Repton and Torksey and searching for these camps could make great metal detecting opportunities. All battles would have involved marching armies and camp sites for both sides.

*Within 15-20 miles of *Burhs* and mint towns. The Burghal Hidage, a ninth-tenth century land tax document lists some 30 *burhs* in Wessex. We don't know the scope of the document and Kent is excluded, despite having several fortified towns. There are over 90 mint towns, which if they weren't *burhs*, would at least have been defended to protect the mint and its associated bullion and coin. A list of mint towns can be found at: http://www.englishhammered.com/anglosaxon/anglosaxon.html

Within a day's walk of these towns, there would have been several Anglo-Saxon settlements, some of which may be lost. To trace such places you could follow all old routes by land and water radiating out from the towns.

*Around places with Viking or Anglo-Saxon names. Many Viking place names end in 'by', 'keld', 'thorpe' or 'toft'. A few useful Anglo-Saxon place-name elements to look out for are 'bury', 'ford', 'ham', 'port' and 'stow'.

http://kepn.nottingham.ac.uk/ has an interactive map of 14,000 place names in England. You can filter by county and by source language to select Anglo-Saxon (Old English) or Viking (Old Norse) place names.

Highwaymen were robbers, usually mounted on horseback, who stole from travellers. These criminals operated from the seventeenth until the late nineteenth century. Highwaymen were called *road agents* in the American West, and *bushrangers* In Australia.

The great age of highwaymen was 1660 to 1714 before an effective police force was in place. Some of them were disbanded soldiers and officers of the English Civil War and French wars. They often attacked coaches and mail carriers and tended to frequent the main coach roads. In England the Bath, Dover, Great North and Oxford Roads were the principle targets.

Research the history of old coach roads in your area to find where highwaymen held up coaches, usually where the coach had to slow at an uphill or winding stretch. A common practice was for highwaymen to hide their loot high up in trees where they could reach from horseback. Over time some or all unrecovered loot could fall out and end up on the ground around the tree. Check out old trees around hold up spots.

Smugglers. When Edward I created a national customs collection system in 1275, principally to finance wars with France, he inadvertently created the smuggler or free-trader as they preferred to be called. Smuggling, or owling, in the medieval period focused on the export of heavily taxed wool, which kept prices artificially low at home. Merchants sometimes smuggled other goods to avoid bans. Grain, for instance, was prohibited from export when prices were high, owing to fears of shortages raising the price of bread and leading to peasant revolts. During the sixteenth century in Bristol and East Anglia the illegal export of grain was a major part of business, with many officials involved, often in collusion with corrupt customs officers.

The introduction of import duties on luxury goods such as tea, wines and spirits, in the mid-seventeenth century transformed smuggling into a 'national sport' involving all classes of society. From 1700 expensive and almost continual wars, mainly with France, led to high rates of duty, as 'war tax', on a growing list of items like lace, silk, and tobacco from continental Europe. Smuggling was a highly profitable venture for poor fishermen, sailors and agricultural labourers (who were employed in landing and distribution operations). In some parts of the country like Kent, Cornwall and the North Riding of Yorkshire, the smuggling industry was more lucrative than legal activities such as farming and fishing.

In 1724-6 Daniel Defoe wrote of Lymington, Hampshire:

"...for though she is very well situated, as to the convenience of shipping, I do not find they have any foreign commerce, except it be what we call smuggling and roguing; which I may say, is the reigning commerce of all this part of the English coast, from the mouth of the Thames to the

Land's End of Cornwall."

While proximity to the continent ensured smuggling activity was at its greatest on the south and east coast, it carried on nationwide. In those days smuggling benefitted almost everyone except the State; the smuggler and his allies profited from the venture and cheaper goods were to be had by all. Despite the lawlessness and occasional dastardly deed perpetrated by smugglers, whose lives were on the line, they were romantically regarded as heroes. Pubs were named after them! Everyone did what seemed good for themselves, resulting in commodities in general demand being imported wholesale, openly and defiantly, along the entire coast of Great Britain, with consequences to the exchequer which can be only imagined.

In 1736 a petition was presented to Parliament by the tea dealers, representing the serious losses they sustained by smuggling. They asserted that nearly half the tea; consumed in England paid no duty. The duty at this time was 4s. (20p) per lb. In December, 1743, a pamphlet was published containing 'A Proposal for Preventing of Running Goods,' and the author observed, "Since an excise of 4s. per lb. was laid on tea, it has brought an average of £130,000 a year into the exchequer, which equates to 650,000 pounds weight of tea. But that the real consumption is vastly greater. Some years ago the treasurer of our East India Company received a letter from Holland intimating that one person in the province of Zealand smuggled yearly for England no less than half a million pounds. Though this seemed incredible, the directors, upon inquiry were convinced of the fact that such a person there was who some few years before had been but an English sailor, was now married to a woman that kept a china shop, and had so well managed affairs that he had four sloops of his own, constantly employed in smuggling; that the quantity of tea which he was supposed to export had not at all been magnified, and that he had more guineas and English coin in his house than any banker in England."

The foreign wars had also kept the army and navy occupied so there were few able men available for the preventive services. The Revenue Cruisers, the Riding Officers and the Preventive Water Guard had to more or less muddle through against a 40,000 strong force of smugglers. The situation didn't improve much after the end of the Napoleonic wars, even with the amalgamation of the three preventive services into the Coastguard, as many demobbed men, who could not find work, took up smuggling. The heyday came to an end in 1839, when customs and excise duties were slashed, simply making smuggling unprofitable.

The smuggled goods themselves are of no real interest to us and besides they will no longer exist in any usable quantity. The real interest is the massive finance involved in buying and selling the goods, which would have been in high denomination gold and silver coin. Guernsey, as other offshore islands, traditionally enjoyed freedom from custom and excise duties and consequently became a distribution centre and a free port to smugglers who could load there without interference. In 1767, the British Government attempted to curb the smuggling by establishing a custom house on Guernsey and prohibiting the supply of dutiable commodities in small packages, which the smugglers needed for their small vessels and landing capabilities. The French Government immediately made several of its ports free to the smugglers, among which was Roscoff, not far from the Channel Islands on the Brittany coast, where several English, Scottish, Irish, and Guernsey merchants established themselves. The Royal Courts of Guernsey protested to the Government that the measures imposed had only shifted smuggling to the enemy (i.e. France), "increasing the population of Brittany and drawing from England some thousands of guineas, which were carried to Paris, which, when brought to Guernsey, were at all times returned to England."

The general condition of the smuggling trade at the commencement of the nineteenth century was fairly well depicted by a pamphlet, which stated that the greater part of the 3,867,500 gallons distilled annually at Schiedam (Rotterdam) was to be smuggled into England; that a distillery had lately been set up for making gin, for the same purpose, at Dunkirk; that the French imported five or six million pounds of tea, the greatest part of which was intended to be smuggled over; that the trade of Dunkirk was mostly carried on by smugglers in vessels not only large but so well constructed for sailing, that seldom one of them was captured; and that the smugglers paid for what they bought in cash, or by the illicit exportation of English wool. It was further given in evidence by the Royal Courts of Guernsey, in the year 1800, that: "there is no doubt that from ten to twelve thousand guineas are every week carried by smugglers to the Continent."

There was a very old man living at Lydd, Kent, who often told how he smuggled gold over to France during the Napoleonic war. He would run across in one of the smuggling galleys, taking a quantity of guineas with him; he could get twenty-five or thirty shillings (in bank notes) for each English guinea (value 21 shillings or £1.05) over there. From further inquiries it seems that this old man, a fisherman by trade, was master of a 12-oared galley during the war, and usually crossed from either Dover or Folkestone to Calais. Having a pass from both English, and French he was never stopped by the men-of-war of either nation. He used to say, that guineas were so plentiful with the smugglers in those days that they used to play pitch and toss with them."

George III gold half-guinea from a beach used by smugglers

There is no doubt that large quantities of valuable coins were crossing our coast between the thirteenth and nineteenth centuries, under circumstances guaranteed to cause losses. The highest cause of loss was the conditions for sailing and landing being much less than ideal. Bad weather and darkness was better for avoiding the preventive men so many cargoes were loaded and landed in rough or foggy weather and usually in the middle of the night. Landing places were generally desolate or inhospitable and routes over cliffs often unsuitable for even mountain goats. Boats were small and sailing risky at the best of times. And whenever people gather for any activity there are bound to be losses.

Smuggling for the most part was a capital offence so the threat of the gallows for being caught lead to many fierce battles with the preventive forces. Many graves in coastal graveyards testify to these clashes and if sites of the action can be discovered there will be finds. Besides losses of single coins there may be purses or even boxes lost. A box of guineas split open after being dropped on Hastings beach, spilling gold coins over the beach was undoubtedly not the only mishap. There is a chance of buried hoards too. Concealed gold coins were left as bribes for Revenue Men which may not have been retrieved. A smuggler could only be convicted if he was caught red-handed and carrying large amounts of coin or having it in the house would be difficult to explain. Notwithstanding the hoarder may have forgotten the place of a hasty burial; many smugglers met an untimely end so there must be a considerable number of smuggler's coin hoards remaining unrecovered.

Smugglers by Morland, George (NMM BHC1077) [Public domain], via Wikimedia Commons

The illegality of smuggling meant that much was carried on in secret so there is little written evidence of smugglers' activities save for those inept enough to get caught. Many older volumes of smuggling history concentrate almost exclusively on the preventive side or customs and excise matters. However there is a growing trend for modern authors to write about smuggling from the law breakers side, rather than the law makers and enforcers; these books will help lead you to find smugglers losses. *The Ordnance Survey Guide to Smugglers' Britain,* by Richard Platt, is an excellent starting point and contains extensive local bibliographies. The book is readily available on the second-hand market for a modest outlay and probably for free at your local library. You should find several local books on smuggling available through your local library or an online search. Learn what you can about smuggling in your area of interest and you should be able to find beaches and the tracks leading from them that will repay your endeavours handsomely.

Stocks, Pillories and Whipping Posts were public restraining devices for minor offences used from the middle ages until the mid-nineteenth century. Stocks held the feet of the person in a sitting position; pillories held the head and wrists of the victim in a standing position while an offender was tied by the wrists upright to a whipping post. In 1351 a law was enacted requiring every town to provide a set of stocks. The length of confinement in these devices amounted to a few hours or a few days but they were regularly occupied and attracted crowds who would delight in throwing rotten fruit and eggs at those constrained in stocks and pillories. These devices were usually sited at market places, village greens or inside and outside churchyards. There is a directory of those known in England here: http://www.pilloryhistory.com/L03Stocks(abridged%20version).pdf

6 DISASTERS

Modern disaster sites resulting in deaths are probably best avoided unless you are invited to search for some specific reason; those involving disruption or loss of property alone may be fair game as will those outside living memory.

Drought. In the past droughts may have caused the loss of settlements through famine but nowadays we have the infrastructure to cope with such events. However water levels fall during droughts and we can gain access to rivers, streams, ponds and lakes that would normally be inaccessible.

Fire will strip vegetation to ground level and make normally inaccessible areas searchable. I well recall a cornfield being accidently set ablaze, which gave me access to the field in searchable condition for many months. The fire had stripped the field down to bare earth but had only destroyed about half the corn seeds, which had to be left to grow again to be ploughed in and then the field replanted with a new crop.

Edward III groat, 1351-61

In the days of open fires in buildings they frequently caught alight, often suffering total destruction. The wealthy and important ones often earned the name 'burnt house', recorded in local histories and newspapers. Salvage of coins and small personal items was rarely thorough so these sites are well-worth searching.

The great fire of Edinburgh, 1824

Floods. Today we have the infrastructure to cope with floods and rescue people affected, even so, flooding can strip vegetation, take down structures, excavate and deposit spoil, offering opportunities when the flooding subsides. Traditionally, people living with flood risk, would have had a safe haven to congregate. Look for high ground around places susceptible to flooding such as those on the coast and in river valleys.

War. The greatest disaster of the twentieth century was World War II, where most of the UK was subjected to aerial bombardment, particularly cities and industrial areas. Rubble disposal is of particular interest as it would contain unrecovered metal objects lost in the blast, although valuables may have been buried in the garden beforehand. Where practical, bomb sites were levelled and landscaped or built over, while excess rubble was used as landfill at pits and quarries nearby. You can determine which pits and quarries disappeared, likely owing to rubble disposal by comparing post-war maps to pre-war maps.

The heaviest bombing by far was in London and much of her rubble was disposed of in the Lea Valley and shipped down the Thames to Kent and Essex. Liverpool was also heavily bombed and her rubble was used as sea defences on nearby Crosby beach but has now been spread by tidal action.

7 HABITATION

Wherever people lived, they lost metal objects so any habitation site is worth a punt. The older, the better, the larger, the better, the wealthier, the better, the more inhabitants the better.

Good indicators of habitation are bricks, masonry, stones, tiles and walls, from boundaries or structures but be aware that broken tile could be from field drainage dating back to medieval times. Crockery, Glass and pottery are other signs of habitation or could be from waste disposal. Crockery is fairly modern but pottery can date back to prehistoric times. As a rule of thumb unglazed black, brown or grey indicates ancient whereas glazed may be medieval to modern. Shells from oysters, mussels and snails, which were eaten by poor people, are another habitation indicator but again could be from waste disposal.

Abandoned Settlements. Thousands of settlements have been abandoned for a variety of reasons. Forces of nature such as floods, drought and coastal erosion have rendered some places uninhabitable; plague and pestilence has decimated populations but often economic and social changes have caused people to move away or a powerful individual, organisation, or government has forced inhabitants to leave. Whatever the reason for abandonment the site may have been occupied with metalwork losers for hundreds of years. You will find a list of some British sites here: https://en.wikipedia.org/wiki/List_of_lost_settlements_in_the_United_Kingdom#References

Many will have been scheduled so you will need to check for that on MAGIC http://www.magic.gov.uk or with your local Finds Liaison Officer and avoid any sites that are. It is still possible to find undiscovered sites fairly easily by looking for crop marks on aerial imagery such as on Google

Earth and LiDAR mapping. There is a Medieval Research Group, which can also help.

Archaeological Barren Sites. Today archaeologists tend to be mainly involved with rescue archaeology as a prelude to construction work but it was not always so. The archaeologist of the not so distant past, up until the 1970s or 1980s was often involved in archaeology for its own sake and would excavate habitation and burial sites for information and to furnish museums with artefacts. Many of these sites became exhausted of finds using the technology of the time and were declared barren. There were no metal detectors to speak of until the 1970s so most of these sites will still hold metal artefacts and repay searching with a metal detector. An easy way to find these sites would be to use ARCHI UK https://www.archiuk.com/ the archaeological finds database and/or explore the transactions of the local archaeological society. There is a risk that some sites will have been scheduled, so you will also need to check for that on MAGIC or with your local Finds Liaison Officer and avoid any sites you find that are scheduled.

Gypsy Camps. The sites of temporary camps of traditional 'Romany' Gypsies would be well worth searching for they earned money from agricultural labouring and selling craft items, which they apparently hoarded in gold sovereigns. They also had rites and ceremonies involving circles of coins. During WWII, camps were set up for the families of Gypsies serving in the forces or involved in essential work; these were closed after the war.

Hamlets & Farmsteads are generally small settlements several hundred years old. The surrounding fields, particularly arable fields, will have seen regular human activity since their establishment. It will be worthwhile to study the history of the settlement and to find how long fields have been arable, if at all, and whether field names indicate any particular use or vanished structure. Tithe maps will be a great help in this respect.

Moats and Trenches. Moats, filled with water were constructed around wealthy and important dwellings like castles and manor houses in medieval times to keep out unwelcome visitors. CBA Research Report #17, *Medieval Moated Sites*, states that there are 5307 known moat sites in England and Wales, of which 401 are scheduled. Moats signify areas where wealthy people lived with high value coins and artefacts to lose. Sites can be found by consulting old large scale Ordnance Survey maps, the Victoria County History series and aerial imagery.

A modern form of moat, although not deliberately water-filled, is trenches dug around fields to stop unauthorised vehicles gaining access to fields. Trenches across fields are also dug for services. You can never tell what may have been uncovered when ground is disturbed like this so never miss an opportunity to search any trenches you can gain access to.

Pounds or Pinfolds. Nearly every village once had its pound or pinfold. A hedged or walled secure area for stray cattle, pigs, geese, etc. to be driven into and impounded at the expense of the owner, until such time as they should pay the fine (the amount claimed by the person on whose land they had strayed, for damage done), and the fee to the pound-keeper, for feeding and watering the livestock. If not claimed in three weeks, the animals were driven to the nearest market and sold, the proceeds going to the impounder and pound-keeper. Many are now derelict or have completely disappeared but their sites may be recorded on old, large scale, Ordnance Survey maps.

Stone Crosses would have probably been in the centre of a settlement originally, if it lies on the outskirts, the settlement may have moved and it could mark the site of an ancient settlement. Nevertheless crosses were gathering and possibly trading places so well worth searching.

Vacant plots. Often the site of a building that has become derelict and demolished but whatever their history they are well worth searching.

Village or Parish Boundaries All villages have a boundary separating from neighbouring villages marked out by man-made or natural features such as tracks, stones, trees, streams and rivers. Land boundaries probably date back to prehistoric times where tribes had a need to protect their habitat and food supply from invaders. No doubt there would be small groups periodically making circuits of their territory to maintain the boundaries and teach the youth, accompanied by much spear waving and chest thumping. This evolved in Roman times into the ceremony of terminalia between villa estates and was taken on by the Church in medieval times as 'beating the bounds'. A formal perambulation of the parish boundaries was usually made on Ascension Day or during Rogation week annually. Knowledge of the limits of each village or parish needed to be handed down to avoid disputes on such matters as liability for upkeep of the church, and burial rights. The parish priest, churchwardens and civic dignities lead a gang of boys armed with sticks who beat the parish boundary markers with them. Sometimes the boys were themselves whipped or bumped on the boundary-stones to improve their memory. Modern mapping has removed the need for such ceremonies although they are still carried out in some places. Finds could be made anywhere along the boundaries but pay particular attention to the areas around markers where more activity took place and possibly hoards were buried.

There is a more compelling reason to take an interest in such boundaries and that is that they took their route for a purpose, following landscape features and respecting property borders. Investigating them can reveal exciting sites just by looking at the land next to the boundary on both sides.

Edward III gold quarter noble, 1351-61 from village boundary

Village Greens and Commons. From 1965 all common land had to be registered which has revealed thousands of plots of land in England and Wales, which may have seen intense human activity for centuries. The average size of a village green is three acres or a little more than one hectare; commons can be much larger. The green was, and may still be, the hub of the village and may have seen markets and fairs, fetes, picnics, sports, stocks, pillories, archery butts and maypoles. Commons traditionally were owned by the lord of the manor and allowed local 'commoners' certain privileges of taking natural produce from the land. In particular: the right to graze livestock; the right to cut and take wood (but not timber), reeds, heather, bracken and so on; the right to dig turf or peat for fuel; the right to take sand, gravel, stone, coal and other minerals and the right to take fish from water. While many commons would not be as potentially exciting as village greens, there would have been a general coming and going which would put losses in the ground.

Through various acts and modifications, rights have evolved to provide a general right of access and recreation, on village and town greens, but unfortunately excluding metal detecting unless permitted by the landowner. Many greens and commons are still in private hands, while others are owned or managed by local councils, often the parish council. Councils, particularly the smaller ones, may be sympathetic to a community project, display of finds in the village hall, etc. There are registers of both greens and commons available:

https://assets.publishing.service.gov.uk/government/uploads/system/uploads/attachment_data/file/218584/village-green-1993.pdf

https://data.gov.uk/dataset/05c61ecc-efa9-4b7f-8fe6-9911afb44e1a/database-of-registered-common-land-in-england

These are not kept up to date but the current register will be held at the local council. Also bear in mind that greens and commons may have contracted or moved and there may be opportunities to search former sites.

8 INDUSTRIAL SITES

Industrial sites date back to the Bronze Age with founders making tools, weapons and jewellery, usually outside of the village so that the furnaces used did not set fire to the dwellings. Iron smelting developed in the Iron Age and continued during the Roman era. The Romans introduced new methods of metal working civil engineering, house-building, and pottery manufacture. Other Roman industries included bone working, carpentry, stonemasonry, textile manufacture, tile making as well as quarrying and mining. The Saxons were not great industrialists, mainly relying on cottage industries. Tile making continued through the medieval period and brick making, glassmaking and papermaking developed from late medieval times. The Industrial Revolution began in the eighteenth century with most cottage industries becoming mechanised processes in factories. Early industries were sited where they could easily get wood for fuel, and/or water for power or process and transport. While coal replaced wood and charcoal for fuel, later industries still required water for power, either directly or for raising steam, and probably for transport and perhaps the process itself. Many industrial sites will be found on watercourses. Britain was at one time the industrial centre of the World but declined in the late twentieth century to a shadow of what it once had been.

Boat, barge and ship building took place from prehistoric times on rivers, creeks and around the coast to furnish the needs of fishing, transport and the Navy.

Brewing and malting. Ale, originally an alcoholic beverage brewed from fermented malted cereal, without hops, has been produced since Roman times in Britain. Ale's pleasant effects were secondary to its original purpose, which was to provide a safe liquid intake, when much of Britain's water was not potable. Ale did not keep well, so brewing was carried out on a domestic scale in homes and inns. The introduction of continental beer in the fifteenth century, using hops with preservative properties, allowed beer to be stored and transported, so by the end of the seventeenth century commercial breweries had almost replaced inn-brewing. In the late nineteenth century restrictive licensing caused the concentration of the industry and the closure of breweries. Malting to supply the brewing industry was traditionally carried out in malt-houses at farms producing grain. The commercialisation of brewing increasingly absorbed the malting process into the breweries.

Brick and tile making was introduced into Britain by the Romans, dying out after their departure to be reintroduced in the middle ages. Owing to the high cost of long distance transport, bricks and tiles were produced on or near construction sites by itinerant makers until the nineteenth century, when developments in canal, rail and road transport and a building boom made dedicated brickworks a going concern. Brick-making declined in some areas owing to exhaustion of brick earth. Of particular interest is the use of domestic rubbish in brick making, which was screened for ash used in the process while the metal (including coins and jewellery) and other unwanted materials was dumped at or near the brickworks.

Chemicals and Pharmaceuticals industries developed from the second half of the eighteenth century. These included manufacture of acids, bleach, tar distillation, agro-chemicals and later pharmaceuticals. The small plants have gradually been swallowed up by conglomerates like ICI.

Cloth and textiles. The woollen industry, organised on the domestic system, until the eighteenth century, has left a legacy of clothiers houses, wool halls and weavers houses. Mechanisation shifted production to Gloucestershire, Lancashire and Yorkshire, which in turn went into decline through foreign competition.

Derelict industrial buildings including garages and shops, particularly in rural locations could make good detecting sites. Where possible search waterways, dumps and grounds. There is a list here:

https://www.derelictplaces.co.uk/main/industrial-sites

Engineering. In the nineteenth century engineering firms and foundries were set up in market centres of agricultural counties to supply farming with iron implements. Other engineering firms developed from millwrights to supply industry needs such as steam engines, paper-making machines and brick and cement making machinery. Traction and plough engines, steam rollers, tram engines and steam wagons were built. Locomotive and carriage works, developed to supply the railways. In the twentieth century engineering evolved into building new products such as petrol and electric lorries, buses, vans, bicycles and motorcycles as well as cables, electrical equipment and aircraft.

Fulling and copperas. Two activities were dependent on the woollen industry. Fulling mills, used fuller's earth to remove oils and grime from woollen cloth.

Copperas works used iron pyrites from fossilized wood gathered from foreshores to produce dyes for textiles as well as ink. However, new dyes produced cheaply near coalfields had destroyed the industry by the early nineteenth century.

Glass-making has been around since Roman times and developed into an important industry in medieval times. Venice was the major European producer initially but England overtook it in the eighteenth and nineteenth centuries. There is still a strong glass industry in the UK but many smaller glass-houses have closed.

Gunpowder. Almost constant warfare in the eighteenth century produced a demand for gunpowder, which carried on during the nineteenth century. Works were sited on waterways for process water, milling and transport. There were often accidental explosions and sites were usually blown-up for security when finished with. By the twentieth century more powerful explosives superseded gunpowder, except for fireworks and antique weaponry. The last British gunpowder factory closed in 1976.

Iron production bloomed in the late sixteenth century particularly in the weald of Kent and Sussex, the Forest of Dean and the Lake District. Furnaces and forges were set up in rural locations having narrow valleys for waterpower for bellows and hammers. Iron ore was dug or mined locally and charcoal from woodlands used for fuel. Producing mainly cannon and shot, the industry consolidated with the introduction of coke fired furnaces in the eighteenth century. Furnace ponds may remain at production sites.

Milling on an industrial scale commenced with Roman watermills to grind grain. The windmill was introduced in the twelfth century and steam power in the nineteenth century. Corn milling by wind and water lasted until the mid-twentieth century, gradually changing to steam power and then closing down as mills in the larger ports such as Liverpool took over. Oil seed crushing, predominantly for paint-making, cooking oil and animal feed, processed locally grown rape and linseed and later imported cotton and rape seed. The industry in the twentieth century concentrated into the British Oil and Cake Mills combine. There are thousands of mill sites throughout Britain, every one worth searching, since transactions would have taken place as people paid the mill for its services.

Navvy camps. The men who worked on improving river navigations for transport from around 1600 were called navigators or navvies for short. Such men were employed on the canal navigations in the 1700s; the railways in the 1800s as well as reservoirs, dams and other large industrial projects. The men came from far and wide to work on these projects, which could last for a number of years and would need some form of accommodation. While some took lodgings nearby, the vast majority lived in wooden huts set up in temporary camps some of which were like villages with church, shops and taverns. While the navvies may have been relatively poorly paid, they would have had metal objects to lose, which would be left in the ground when the camp was dismantled. There would probably be a dump also. A tip for finding railway navvy camps is to examine a 1950s Ordnance Survey map which will show all nineteenth century railway lines constructed in the area covered by the map. Look for sites of major works such as deep cuttings, long embankments, tunnels and bridges, especially those in rural areas. The usual arrangement was to make a camp at each end of the construction, the navvies working towards each other. Search any accessible ground around both ends of the works.

Part of Scar Village camp which housed over 1000 navvies during construction of Scar House Reservoir between 1921 and 1936. Image by David Pickersgill and licensed for reuse under the Creative Commons Attribution-ShareAlike 2.0 license

Lime and cement. Lime was burnt for the London and local building markets from the seventeenth century. By the mid-nineteenth century lime was being replaced by stronger Portland cement for building purposes.

Waterside locations facilitated barge transport to the London market and docks, and the carriage of raw materials, chalk, river mud high in silica and alumina. At the peak of production, in 1900, works on the Thames and Medway produced about two thirds of England's cement. The introduction of new technology rotary kilns and increased foreign competition led to concentration of the industry and closure of works.

Mining and Quarrying. The United Kingdom has a rich history of mining and quarrying. Non-ferrous minerals, particularly copper and tin, have been mined since the Bronze Age. Copper has been mined in Wales for over 4000 years. Lead and copper attracted the Romans to Britain. The Romans introduced iron tools and used local slaves to mine galena ore, from deep mines located in Scotland and Wales which produced lead, tin and silver.

Widespread availability of coal and iron spawned the Industrial Revolution of the eighteenth and nineteenth centuries. Coal and iron ore were once mined in large quantities in the UK and used for steel and energy production. In the twentieth century, production of coal and metals declined owing to foreign competition.

Building and construction materials industries have left the biggest impact on the landscape in the form of quarries, chalk, clay and sand pits. Stone has been quarried for centuries. Stone came back into fashion in the nineteenth century for use on public buildings, and was used in the twentieth century for roads. As well as workers losing metal objects and the possibility of camps for short term projects, it was common practice to fill abandoned workings with domestic refuse, the earlier of which will be well rotted down and now worth searching or digging for relics. The extraction of aggregates has increased in recent times and the practice now is to remove and save the topsoil and subsoil. When the working has been depleted, the hole is filled up with inert material and topped off with subsoil and topsoil, with the majority of metal objects still mixed in. So do not be put off searching a field because of former material extraction.

Papermaking began in a large scale in the sixteenth century, usually sited on rivers and sometimes re-using redundant fulling mills. The raw material was initially rag from industrial centres often brought in by barge. In the second half of the nineteenth century wood pulp from Scandinavia began replacing rag.

Large gilded silver medal recovered from paper mill waste

Railway fences. Trains have always attracted young and old alike, especially in the age of steam and enthusiasts have tended to be drawn to fences to watch the trains and record numbers.

Railways (disused). While there have been closures of unprofitable railways in the UK from Victorian times onwards, the greatest was a result of the Beeching Axe of 1963 which identified 2,363 stations and 5,000 miles (8,000 km) of railway line for closure. As a result vast areas of previously unavailable land has been released for exploration. Railway stations, tracks, sidings, junctions and cuttings were all closed, some were returned to agriculture or turned into cycle paths but many were just left and may be overgrown but searchable to a greater or lesser extent. If you consider that hundreds of workmen were used to construct and maintain the railway there are bound to be metal losses. There is also a possibility of older material disturbed in construction: the London, Chatham and Dover Railway ran through a rich Anglo-Saxon cemetery at Faversham in Kent. It is true that there will be plenty of nuts, bolts and other engineering debris but there is a good chance of discovering metal signs and other railway memorabilia that are very collectable.

Reclaimed land. Land reclamation schemes have existed since Saxon times. Often the early schemes involved reclaiming land from the sea or rivers, where metal objects deposited in water may now be found on land. More recent schemes may have involved importing topsoil from who knows where, so always worth a look.

Salt. Over thousands of years prehistoric man learned the use of salt for preserving food, curing hides and healing wounds. In the Bronze and Iron Ages solid salt was obtained by evaporating seawater and brine, from springs, in pottery vessels. The Romans developed industrial scale salt pans at coastal sites and brine springs in the 'wich' towns of Cheshire and Worcestershire, principally to supply the army. The primary evaporation was carried out in bays using the Sun, with final evaporation in lead pans heated by wood fires. The technology continued with little change during the Anglo Saxon and medieval period but note that many coastal sites in East Anglia are now several miles inland owing to the Fens being drained. Salt ways also developed for moving the salt overland. By the sixteenth century Scotland was producing a considerable amount of salt from seawater using sea coal as fuel and iron pans. By 1620 the cost of wood for fuel was becoming prohibitive and salt works were switching to coal, which tended to melt the lead pans so there was a switch to iron pans as well. Rock salt was discovered in Cheshire in 1670 and within 20 years a number of pits had been established. Meanwhile the coastal sites still flourished. In 1702 the Salt Act imposed a tax on salt and prohibited new salt works on the British mainland outside of Cheshire. Ireland however was exempt and this generated a boom in Irish salt production from coastal sites and a decline in mainland salt production outside Cheshire. Salt was at this time being used for butter-making and salted fish and meat. The canals and railways improved Cheshire's ability to supply London and southern markets. Consolidation of the industry followed in the late nineteenth century leaving the Cheshire area as the surviving UK salt industry.

Tanning. Tanneries were established at most market towns to supply leather for industrial and domestic needs. Cheap imports and new materials reduced demand after World War I causing the industry to greatly decline.

Utilities. Public utilities: gasworks, waterworks and power stations were established from the nineteenth century; many have closed.

Warehousing. Warehouse buildings date from the sixteenth century.

9 LANDSCAPE

Barrows & Mounds. Barrows, often labelled tumuli on early maps, are mounds of earth (or stone cairns) of varying shapes and sizes that were built from 3800BC to 800AD. Known barrows are normally scheduled and out of bounds to metal detecting but few barrows survive intact and many have been ploughed-out and may be accessible, with permission. Whether the barrow is scheduled or not, accessible unscheduled surroundings for up to half a mile will be worth searching as they will have been revered and visited throughout history and possibly reused for a variety of functions.

Sutton Hoo. Photo: Amitchell125 at English Wikipedia, CC BY-SA 3.0 <https://creativecommons.org/licenses/by-sa/3.0>, via Wikimedia Commons

Beacon Sites. Notwithstanding signal fires had been lit on hilltops for centuries, Elizabeth I passed a law requiring county officials to maintain unlit bonfires on prominent hilltops. The fires were to be lit if England's security was threatened by invasion. The beacons were certainly ignited in 1588 when the Spanish Armada was sighted, signalling the militia to march south and sailors to board their ships. Several invasions since probably resulted in further beacon fires but in the eighteenth century, the Admiralty replaced some of the beacons with a network of manned semaphore stations eight miles apart in line of sight. These signalling devices endured for around 100 years before becoming obsolete with the introduction of the electric telegraph. Many of the hills used were named beacon hill, bonfire hill, or telegraph hill. In 1988, in celebration of 400 years since the defeat of the Spanish Armada, beacons in the form of a metal basket on a large pole were once again set up on prominent hills and are still there today. Whether the original beacon hill has been selected or not would be worth investigating with a metal detector.

Forest and Woodland make up about 10% of the land in Great Britain and has considerable potential for metal detecting for much ancient woodland has seen activity for centuries in harvesting wood for building, charcoal, fencing, and kindle; grazing pigs; hiding of valuables and shelter for fugitives, robbers and smugglers. Quite often sites of early industry and substantial former homes will be hidden in woodland and well worth searching.

Most of Britain was originally covered in dense woodland and has since been either cleared or managed by man. A large number of species could signify ancient woodland. Oaks were grown well spaced out to be used for shipbuilding. Coppicing was and still remains common, where every ten years or so trees are cut down for timber. Animals, particularly pigs, were grazed in woods and forests but they eat young shoots unless fenced off. To avoid animal damage, pollarding was developed where pruning encouraged several trunks to grow from halfway up the main trunk. Coppicing and pollarding of usually hazel, willow, ash, encouraged the trees to produce bunches of tall straight thin flexible stems ideal for wattle making. Demand for wattle was enormous for houses, fencing and military shields against arrows. Charcoal burning was another major woodland industry. Woodsmen lived on the site in crude shelters for season after season losing tools and coins, etc. Clearings could be the remains of these or other buildings. Well-trodden tracks radiated out to village, castle, and manor house. Search under bushes besides tracks where often objects end up. Place name elements such as ley or leigh (clearing); ett (small enclosure) and sele (willow) may give clues to sites.

Check out woods near pubs where patrons may have ventured into the woods to sleep it off and also for courting. They did not venture far into the woods. The best sites around popular pubs can often be spotted from old photos and real photograph postcards, which can be found on the internet, collector's fairs, etc.

Look for boundaries such as a definite line of trees, banks, and ditches. Search them well.

Hoards were often secreted in hollow trees in woods which gave cover from prying eyes. Search the trunk, low branches, exposed roots, and surrounding area. Search large fallen logs where people may have sat and children played. Crevices may have coins or trinkets poked into them. Search paths, streams, stiles, and prominent trees.

Royal forests were reserved for the king's hunting. William I had settlements in such forests destroyed without notice.

Rhododendrons are not indigenous but were introduced in Victorian times for game-bird cover. Snowdrops escaped from abbey gardens.

The Forestry Commission manages some 700,000 hectares (1.7M acres) of land in England and Scotland, unfortunately, they only allow metal detecting on archaeological projects. Nevertheless, there are many parcels of woodland in private ownership where metal detecting permission could be obtained. Woodland is generally available for searching all year round, offering some protection from high winds, rain, and snow. And in freezing conditions, woodland floors rarely become frozen solid. The major drawback in deciduous and mixed woodland is the build-up of decayed leaves, which deeply covers older losses (but leaves blow away on isolated or small clumps of trees), and the soil acidity around conifers rapidly corrodes most buried metals. In summer thick undergrowth can inhibit searching and you will need a copious supply of insect repellent (or perhaps a beekeeper's outfit) to avoid being eaten alive.

Hedges or former hedge lines. Hedges were planted by people to mark a boundary or to keep animals in or out. Many hedges started their lives off as banks or as fences of cut sticks (some of which took root). Hedges were often used to bury or conceal valuables and people would frequently sit beside them for shelter from sun and wind. The downside, especially with roadside hedges, is that they attract a lot of junk. Nevertheless, perseverance pays. It is useful to be able to date a hedge to give some idea of the length of time it has been in use. The rule of thumb is: measure out a 30 metre length of hedge and work along the hedge systematically counting each woody species; repeat this process with two or three different 30 metre sections of the hedge; calculate the average number of woody species per 30 metre section and multiply by one hundred years.

Trees, especially large and old trees are a landmark and a perfect place to hide something under or nearby such as a hoard. However, the tree needs to have been reasonably accessible by people, at least for a good part of its life.

You can judge a tree's age by the diameter of its trunk; most species expand at approximately one inch per year. Measure the circumference with a tape at breast height and divide by three to get the diameter. If there is a cut or fallen tree nearby of similar size you can count the annular rings which are produced at the rate of one per year. Look also for tree rings where a dying tree sends up new growth around the trunk and the original tree dies and rots away leaving a ring of new trunks that may be several hundred years old.

Yew trees were introduced by the Romans and can live up to 3000 years; chestnut up to 1000 years; oak up to 900 years; ash up to 700 years; sycamore and beech up to 300 years. Many old trees will have died, been felled, or reduced to stumps which would repay searching as they may have seen use during their lifetimes.

Oak trees tend to contain hollows sometimes used for concealment and are most famous for hiding treasure. Never miss an oak or yew tree particularly if hollow. There were gospel oaks used for preaching at religious meets and marriage oaks where couples married and attendees threw money at them. Elms no longer reach maturity owing to Dutch elm disease but had similar hollows to oaks for concealment. They were almost as popular as oaks for hiding treasure, however, as none are now standing you would need to find their site.

Lime leaves were a popular early animal fodder.

Sycamores were often used for hanging.

The area beneath Horse Chestnut (conker) trees, where schoolboys spend a lot of time trying to get the conkers down from the branches, is always worth a special search. While dodging the returning sticks from their friends it is not too difficult to lose items. Search under the whole area of the branches.

Tradition has it that a person burying treasure would plant a hawthorn on top of it.

Trees were used for mile markers and like bus stops were favoured as meeting places for horsemen, tramps, coaches, etc. Mile trees were replaced with milestones from 1720. Mile numbering on early maps may coincide with these trees. Roadside trees particularly oak were used by toll collectors. Before turnpikes became established, the upkeep of roads was the landowner's responsibility and they collected tolls. It was fairly common for coins to be just thrown in the direction of the toll collector rather than stopping for an official handover. Single parkland trees were a magnet for children playing, parents, picnickers, and lovers. Trees acted as markers for hundred and shire meeting places. Hundred courts were usually beneath an oak, ash, beech or chestnut. They were sometimes called tort trees which may be remembered in trees or woods having tort in their name.

Bulla of Pope Nicholas IIII, 1288-92, from 'Hundred Beech' site

Cockfighting and prize-fighting, pagan worship, and other events were probably advertised by reference to a venerable tree at the site. Fairlop Oak for instance marked the site of a fair. While former well-known trees have probably disappeared they may be recorded in local histories and place names. Ordnance Survey maps show villages named for trees such as Sevenoaks. Look for Saxon banks and ditches in the vicinity.

10 MEETING SITES

From the time man formed tribes and communities, there became a need for rules or laws and administration or government for the greater good. The tried and tested method for establishing the laws and government of groups of people, large and small, is the meeting. The word is derived from Saxon 'moot' and Norse 'Thing', forming the 'mot thing' or assembly of freeholders. From ancient times these meetings were held in the open air, owing both to a lack of suitable accommodation and because of superstitious belief that meetings must be held under heaven or the sun. Many of these meetings took place at ancient sites and have been little studied, so no one knows what other activities went on, such as markets and fairs, revenue collection, entertainment or religious ceremonies. You can be certain of plenty of lost metal objects though!

Popular places for holding meetings were generally either defensible or secret. By far the largest groups of places were mountains and hills. Another large group of meetings took place by or under the boughs of trees. Many other meetings took place near water. Megaliths were another favourite meeting place: near large standing stones, within stone circles, at great burial places, caves and tombs. And a few assemblies took place at the chief's residence, on large open plains and in contrast an enclosed paddock.

Before the Romans came in 43 AD, the native population would have held their meetings at most of the places above that existed in Britain at the time. Rome was an advanced civilisation, which held a different view on life. The Romans built towns and held most of their meetings in the central forum. Celtic tradition would have felt the civilising influences of the Roman presence, as would the Saxons who followed. And once the Roman legions had gone they left behind buildings, which became used as more landmarks for meetings. People met outside city gates or outside the church doors, in the churchyard or monastery courtyard, in the market place and in paved areas.

By the late eleventh century, the British Isles had been divided up into territorial units, most or all of which would have held a court or meeting. The largest were the countries: England, Ireland, Scotland and Wales. Apart from a few large provincial divisions, such as north and south, highlands and lowlands, next came the counties or shires with the shire-reeve or sheriff responsible for administration and justice. The counties were divided into units called hundreds in most of England and Wales (Wales had commots before the sixteenth century) but also Wapentakes (Yorkshire) and Wards (Cumberland, Durham and Northumberland). The hundred may have originally represented an area containing one hundred 'families' or households. A few counties had larger divisions containing several hundreds or their equivalent such as the lathes of Kent, the rapes of Sussex and the ridings of Yorkshire.

The hundred court was the principle local administrative and judicial unit in England and Wales until the nineteenth century. In Scotland the equivalent to the hundred was the parish and in Ireland, the barony. Way back in time the head of household was the lord of the family and responsible for the actions of everyone in the family including its slaves. Three wealthy lords for every medieval tithing or vill (parishes after the sixteenth century) comprising the hundreds, had to attend the court meetings held every three weeks.

In general the hundred (or its equivalent) was named after the meeting place so you may learn much just by analysing the name. As a start you need to know the names of the hundreds, but these are easy to find. On the Internet you can visit:

http://en.wikipedia.org/wiki/List_of_hundreds_of_England_and_Wales
or just Google (name of county) + hundreds or parishes or baronies, etc. In the traditional world, many Victorian and earlier county maps list or name hundreds as do local histories and gazetteers of the same periods. **Successful Detecting Sites**, (Greenlight Publishing) provides maps or lists of English and Welsh hundreds, Scottish Parishes and Northern Ireland baronies as well as more information identifying many meeting sites.

Popular name elements associated with meeting places are:

Barrow is a relatively small artificial burial mound, usually round (but can be linear as long barrow). Round barrow(s) can also be called a tumulus or tumuli.

Berga, Borough is a smooth rounded usually natural hill but can be a barrow.

Beria, Bury is a hill fort but may refer to any fortified building or natural feature that has the appearance of fortification.

Bridge is a river crossing.

Clif, Cliff, Cliffe, Clive is a hill, ridge or headland with a vertical or near vertical face. These are found on the coast and in inland valleys.

Don, Down, Dun is a low flat-topped hill often with a settlement on the summit and sometimes a fort.

Ford is a river crossing.

Gate can be a city gate but is more often a road, usually Roman or earlier.

Hoe, Ho, Hoo, O, Oe, Ow is a hill-spur, a projecting raised piece of land usually rising to a point and falling with a concave slope.

How, Hou is a round barrow.

Law, Lo, Loe, Low is an artificial mound, it may be a re-used burial mound but often constructed specifically for meetings.

Le, Lea, Leigh, Ley from the eighth century indicated forest, wood, glade, clearing and from the tenth century meant pasture or meadow.

Stane, Ston, Stone, Stow, Stowe refer to standing stones.

Tree refers to a tree and species (ash, elm, oak, etc.) or numbers may be added or substituted.

Twy means two.

Finding the meeting site is not so easy, but often there will be features at or near the site either named 'hundred' or given the name of the particular hundred. People from all over the hundred needed to get to meetings, so the site would be fairly centrally located within the hundred and would be accessible by road (Roman or earlier), waterway or both.

I have only searched one meeting site, which nevertheless has kept me going with interesting finds for many years and is still producing. The clues were that the hundred name element *borough* suggested the meeting place to be a natural hill. On top of a quite central particular hill, a wood bore the name of the hundred. An ancient long-distance track-way and a former navigable river ran close to the hill. There used to stand an old tree hereabouts called 'The Hundred Beech', which established a field forming a large part of the side of the hill, at the union of two parish boundaries as a hundred meeting place or at least part of it.

The first time I searched this field it was remarkably lacking in finds, for other than modern spent ammunition cases I only found a small Tudor belt fitting, welcome nevertheless. The second short search wasn't looking any better until as the light was failing I headed for the gate to be stopped in my tracks by a crisp signal. I dug up a small green disk, I thought to be Roman, although the coin felt rather too thick. I washed the coin carefully at home and could just make out the head of Apollo on one side and an eagle on the other. The coin was an Iron Age Unit of Eppillus around 2000 years old.

The following weekend I returned to the same field, again the finds were few but I was delighted to recover a Thurrock type Potin and a medieval buckle. This field was definitely getting interesting and fortunately the field was being left fallow for a few months, giving me time for a thorough search.

I started at the top of the field where most of the finds had surfaced and fairly quickly built up a collection of medieval buckles, loom weights, spindle whorls and thimbles. Further down the field, the buckles, weights and whorls still kept coming, but the accompanying finds changed to jettons. Occasionally something different surfaced: a cut halfpenny of Henry I, a medieval strap junction decorated with a face, a papal bulla and a casket key. The crowning glory initially appeared to be a washer but on turning it over, the glint of gold was unmistakable. Gentle washing off-site showed a gilded silver ring brooch, inscribed with the letters IESVSX (Jesus Christ), unfortunately missing most of its original sword shaped pin, broken off at the hilt. I also found two silver coins within a metre of the brooch albeit both in a poor state. I reported the brooch and two coins as a potential treasure find, which was eventually disclaimed.

Medieval gilded silver ring brooch (pin digitally restored)

The brooch was the last of the exceptional finds from the field until the plough produced a fresh metallic crop. Surprisingly, considering the scarcity of coinage here, the first day on the ploughed field, I picked up from the surface a superb groat of Edward III followed a little later by two Tudor coins and a dress hook. The buckles, coins, jettons, weights and whorls still kept coming, maintaining my interest while I waited for something more unusual. A small circular mount showing a squirrel, a strap end, and a horse harness pendant were all very welcome and almost the last recovery of the season was a lead personal seal matrix inscribed S[IGILLUM] ROB[ER]TI FILII HAMON[IS] (Seal of Robert son of Eamon) around an eight pointed star.

The search of this site has been an interesting experience, which convinced me that hundred meeting places are well worth seeking as successful detecting sites.

Court Sites As well as hundred courts and shire courts there were many other open-air courts such as court Leets and courts Baron which were mainly concerned with manorial rights. Derbyshire lead miners were controlled by the Great Barmote courts. Tin miners of the West Country had Stannary courts which met at Crockern Tor near Princetown, Devon. There were Lawless courts which met at King's Hill, Rochford, Essex and another met at Epping under a maple tree. The Wroth Silver court has for some 800 years compelled representatives of the 25 parishes of Knightlow hundred to pay dues annually at Knightlow cross (remains), on Knightlow Hill, near Rugby, Warwickshire. The once powerful Cinque Ports Confederation met at the site now marked by Shepway Cross, Lympne, Kent.

Crosses. There were several types of cross but all were a landmark and a magnet for people. There were memorial crosses such as Eleanor crosses. King Edward I and Queen Eleanor of Castile had been married for 36 years and she stayed by the King's side throughout his many travels. While on a royal progress, she died in the East Midlands in November 1290. Edward erected the crosses in her memory, to mark the nightly resting-places along the route taken, while transporting her body to Westminster Abbey, London. Market crosses, some covered, marked market sites. Boundary crosses marked limits of parishes and manors. Sanctuary crosses were erected for travellers passing through dense woods, which were respected by robbers, providing the potential victim reached the cross first. A great number of preaching crosses were erected to mark where preaching took place ahead of church building. Most are in the west and south, as the earliest preachers came from Ireland. A fair few are near ancient wells and pagan sites which promoted continuity of religion. Weeping crosses were erected for use of those compelled to do penance by the clergy. Some mark the site of a battle or other event. Cross-roads were held sacred and had a small stone erected marked with a cross. At least five thousand existed in England but many were damaged or destroyed by puritans in the seventeenth century. A few stone crosses survive and sites of others can be located by place name and local history research. See: Alfred Rimmer, *Ancient Stone Crosses of England*, (London, 1875).

Moorland cross. Image by fsHH from Pixabay.com

Temperance meetings and processions took place where revellers were ripe for conversion. Such meetings at Thornton Abbey in Yorkshire attracted 19,000 people. Check Methodist archives and temperance society proceedings.

11 MILITARY AND SIMILAR SITES

Military badges, nineteenth-twentieth centuries

Airfields. There were hundreds of airfields established during World War II many of which are now disused. Start your research with the interactive map at:

https://www.rotary-ribi.org/clubs/page.php?PgID=632446&ClubID=460

Archery Butts & Shooting Ranges. The first Medieval Archery Law was passed in 1252 when all Englishmen between the ages of 15 and 60 years were ordered, to equip themselves with a bow and arrows. In 1363 the second archery Law mandated Englishmen to practise their skills with the longbow every Sunday! Special places called Butts were designated for archery training. The Butts were usually located on the greens of villages or towns or on common land or just outside the settlement. The name butts may occur in field and place names leaving a clue to the location. As well as casual losses from the activity it was not unusual for archers to place a coin on the ground to mark the toe line, the better-off may have used gold coins!

In the sixteenth century the longbow was superseded by the musket and later the rifle. Training was still very necessary in the use of firearms and it is likely that the militia used the archery butts for shooting practice. As the range of firearms increased it probably became necessary to re-locate ranges well away from settlements. Target rifle shooting became a popular sport in the eighteenth century as did the forerunner of clay pigeon shooting where, on ranges, the gentry shot real pigeons released from cages. Archery also saw a revival in the eighteenth century using the rifle ranges. With the constant threat of foreign invasion during the nineteenth century, rifle ranges appear in some profusion on Victorian Ordnance Survey maps. Modern archery sites may also be worth searching as well as yielding modern coins they could lie on an old site. The offer of recovering lost arrows may encourage permission.

Barracks. See: *Map of Great Britain, shewing all the barracks*, 1807 https://maps.nls.uk/view/216587068

Battle Sites. Most known sites of the actual battle will be protected but organised metal detecting surveys are undertaken. See: http://www.battlefieldstrust.com/default.asp Most battles would have involved marching armies and camp sites for both sides, which may be searchable. Bear in mind that the armies marched mainly on roads existing at the time. A list of battles is given on The Battlefields Trust website (above) and in: *How to Find Britain's Buried Treasure Hoards* (Greenlight, 2017) For more detail see: David Smurthwaite, *The Complete Guide to the Battlefields of Britain*, (London, 1993).

Boy Scouts, Girl Guides and similar groups. The main interest for us is that they organised regular outdoor camps in the countryside. While these developed in the late twentieth century into more or less fixed camps with amenities such as toilets and shower blocks (still worth searching): https://campsites.scouts.org.uk/sites it was not always so. From their formation in the late nineteenth to early twentieth century it was the job of the scoutmaster or their equivalent leader to arrange suitable campsites with landowners. According to D Francis Morgan in *Standing Camps,* (1938), the following needed to be taken into account for a successful camp:

*Interest and romance of the site.

*Elevation and Drainage.

*View.

*Space and ground for games.

*Soil and vegetation.

*Protection from wind, storms and sun.

*Freedom from human and animal intervention.

*Accessibility for transport, equipment and supplies.

*Water for cooking, washing and bathing.

*Wood for fuel for cooking and camp fires.

Once a successful site had been found it would have been used regularly and there will be plenty of losses. Local knowledge will help in locating such sites that may well have developed into modern camp sites.

The Boys Brigade founded 1883, have their annual camp at Glynde, Sussex. There are other camps around the country: https://boys-brigade.org.uk/bb-gazette/approved-campsites/

Civil War sieges. Such sites tend to be neglected and may offer better access and pickings than battle sites. A useful book is Peter Young & Wilfrid Emberton, *Sieges of the Great Civil War, 1642-1646,* (London, 1978)

Civil War skirmishes. There were many skirmishes in the civil war which you may find from local histories if you know what regiments got up to when major battles took place. Concentrate on churchyards, small manor houses, river crossings and road junctions within five miles around sites of major events.

Georgian and Victorian military sites An enormous amount of military activity has taken place in the British Isles over the centuries through almost continuous internal and external strife. Although many battles were fought on foreign soil, transit camps training grounds and stations were in Britain. Military camps abounded in great numbers particularly in the south near the Continent. Documentation of the exact whereabouts of camps is hard to find as locations were kept secret but may be preserved in folklore. Camps would be on or near to high ground for defence, often on commons, and may be open or wooded. It is likely that at least one public house would be close by and there may be track ways leading to or through the site. Victorian rifle ranges would be sited nearby and these are clearly marked on old large scale Ordnance Survey maps. The military used navigable rivers for transport. Foreshores near military installations, whether standing or not, will repay searching.

Gun Emplacements. The development of cannons had made traditional castles largely obsolete by the sixteenth century. To combat the new weaponry the philosophy was to build a small target equipped with a large gun or guns. Local lords and communities were traditionally responsible for coastal defences but the threat of French and Spanish invasion led Henry VIII to order a major programme of work between 1539 and 1547 called a "device". The Device Forts and blockhouses were a series of gun emplacements built to defend the English and Welsh coast. The fortifications ranged from large stone castles to protect the Downs anchorage in Kent, to small blockhouses overlooking Milford Haven, Pembrokeshire, and earthwork bulwarks along the Essex coast. These fortifications were equipped with cannons, intended to fire on enemy shipping to prevent forces being landed or English and allied ships being attacked in harbour. The Device Forts saw hardly any action before the peace treaty of 1546. A little later, some defences were abandoned and decommissioned. After war broke out with Spain in 1569, Elizabeth I had heavy cannons positioned along the south coast to protect potential landing sites from invaders. Although a few were set up in existing fortifications like Pevensey and Camber, most of these were established on new sites accompanied by earthworks and trench systems. Recorded emplacements are Selsea, Dell, Pagham, Littlehampton, Kingston, Goring, Lancing, Shoreham, Hove, Brighton, Newhaven, Bletchington, Bishopstone, Seaford, Chinting Farm, Cuckmere Haven, Birling Gap, Bourne, Cooden, Bulverhythe, Hastings, Fairlight, Winchelsea and Rye.

By the end of the century, the defences were badly out of date and in the early seventeenth century many of the forts were left to decay. Most of the fortifications saw service in the English Civil Wars during the 1640s and were garrisoned during the Commonwealth, continuing to form England's major coastal defences against the Dutch after Charles II was restored in 1660. Again left to decay during the eighteenth century, but from the time of the French Revolutionary Wars onwards many of the Device Forts were modernised and re-armed. Additionally Martello towers, small defensive, mainly coastal, forts were built across the British Empire during the nineteenth century (103 in Britain). The Martello towers were used during the first half of the nineteenth century, but became obsolete with the introduction of powerful rifled artillery. Many were taken over by the Coastguard to combat smuggling.

There were fears over possible French invasion throughout the nineteenth century, which produced investment in Device Forts still thought to be militarily valuable, and encouraged the decommissioning of others. In the 1860s, during Lord Palmerston's premiership, there was another spate of tower and fort building. The Palmerston Forts (or Follies, as they saw no action) are circular and resemble Martello towers.

By the twentieth century, developments in warfare had made almost all of the remaining Device Forts obsolete in modern coastal defence. During the First and Second World Wars they were rearmed and saw action against the German Luftwaffe aircraft. In the 1950s the fortifications were considered redundant and decommissioned for good. Coastal erosion over the centuries has extensively damaged or completely destroyed some sites. Fifteen Martello towers were demolished for masonry; the sea washed thirty away and four were destroyed in military experiments. Forty-seven Martello towers survive in England, a few of which have been converted into museums or private residences but most are derelict.

https://www.geograph.org.uk/article/Martello-Towers

https://en.wikipedia.org/wiki/List_of_forts

http://anti-aircraft.co.uk/HAA_gun_sites_map.html

Marching armies. The Romans were effectively the first army in Britain and using the existing road system as much as possible, marched forward one day at a time covering 10-20 miles depending on terrain. At the end of a day's march they had to build a defensive camp or miniature fort within which they would pitch their leather tents. They dug a perimeter ditch and piled the extracted earth up behind the ditch to form a rampart which they embellished with sharpened stakes, points upwards and outwards. The Romans modified and improved the road system and by the time they left, their road system remained much the same until the turnpike roads began in the late seventeenth century. So subsequent armies marched on the Roman road system and made camps as the Romans did although not to any particular pattern. A few armies used the sea and navigable rivers. The Great Heathen Army travelled England for 14 years, which would have required many temporary camps. Vikings did not build temporary forts like the Romans so have left no clear trace in the landscape. However they did make camp for the winter in several places such as Thetford, Repton and Torksey and searching for these camps could make great metal detecting opportunities.

Military Camps, Cantonment (garrison) Sites and Mustering Areas. Tented Encampments are not well documented but a few in the south of England, 1596-1639 are: Bosham, Royal Heath, Bury Hill, Arundel, Warning Camp, Ashington, Steyning, Ditchling, Haywards Heath, Brighton, Tarring, Lewis, Uckfield, Alciston, Berwick, Alfriston, Hastings, Battle. Militia or Regimental camps, 1776-1815 are: Ashdown Forest, Brighton, Broadwater Forest, Coxheath, Warley Common (Essex). Early military camps were often set up around ancient inns flanking important routes. To identify camp sites in the landscape, look for large (football size) stones or rocks in a rectangle or circle pattern used as tent 'pegs' and possibly U shaped ditches and raised platforms from bedding. Circular earth mounds 15-20 feet diameter and several feet high may be remains of ovens and look similar to barrows.

There were also camp sites for the armies during the two World wars. Check local newspapers. The Archaeology Data Service has free downloadable files on camps between 1858 and 2000:

https://archaeologydataservice.ac.uk/archives/view/armycamp_eh_2006/overview.cfm

Pillboxes. In 1940, the War Office laid plans to provide a number of basic but effective pillbox designs mainly as rifle and light machine gun posts, that could be constructed by soldiers and local labour at appropriate defensive locations. It is estimated that some 28,000 pillboxes and other hardened field fortifications were constructed in the United Kingdom, of which about 6,500 survive. In the late 1970s, journalist Henry Wills began research on the topic, publishing: *Pillboxes: A Study of UK Defences* (1985). Interest was stimulated, culminating in the Defence of Britain Project, attempting to record all known military defence sites.

https://archaeologydataservice.ac.uk/archives/view/dob/download.cfm

https://en.wikipedia.org/wiki/List_of_World_War_II_prisoner-of-war_camps_in_the_United_Kingdom

12 PARKS AND GARDENS

Allotments can usually be found with ease and having been used often for over 200 years, finds soon build up. On old sites there will be coins and artefacts deposited with nightsoil or rag waste. There will be recent losses too as the activity tends to deposit objects in the ground with reckless abandon. One way of getting into allotments is to advertise your finding service for jewellery, tools, etc, with allotment associations. Several hoards have already been found on such sites, most buried during the Second World War when there was the threat of losing your money if it was in your house when bombed. If there is an area of allotments which are no longer in use, contact the landowner for search permission. For allotments still in use you will need permission from the landowner and each plot tenant, unless searching for the tenant's own property.

A typical allotment

George I shilling

Gardens. For most of us, our own land will consist of a garden or yard of some sort, which is nevertheless a very good place to start. Gardens will have seen much human activity in a relatively small area: gardening, sunbathing, alfresco meals, children playing, etc. Not to mention the possibility of metallic losses from whatever took place before the garden was laid out. I remember finding over 50 coins in my mother-in-law's small 1920s garden and my most valuable single find, a Tudor iconographic gold ring, came from the garden of a thirteenth century house. So check out your garden and any other land you or your family owns or rents perhaps, although strictly you should obtain permission from the landowner if searching rented land as the landowner can claim any ownerless objects you may find. However if you are the occupier of the land such as a garden or you have an allotment, for instance, the landowner is unlikely to object.

Having searched your own land you will have a few finds to show and will undoubtedly be able to find relatives, friends, neighbours and colleagues willing to allow you to search their land also, for a share in the finds. This simple approach of asking anyone and everyone you know could keep you busy with sites for quite some time. Gardens yield more gold and silver finds than fields and wrecks it seems. You need to work very neatly on other peoples gardens, there is an argument between using a spade or small hand tools for finds extraction, whichever you can work neatest with is best, but you may want to let the landowner make the choice. Use a polythene bag, drop-cloth or Frisbee to deposit the plug and excavated earth onto so you can put it all back in the hole without leaving a brown stain. Either avoid digging in dry weather or douse your filled holes with water.

Pay attention to:

*Abandoned Houses and Structures

*Clothes Lines

*Outhouses, sheds, greenhouses, etc.

*Seats

*Sundial Sites. Perhaps one in ten villas built in England between 1890-1914 had a sundial, most were sited in gardens on an area of paving with cracks that trap valuables. Many have been grassed over. Large scale Ordnance Survey maps may show these.

*Walls

*Wells

Public Parks, open spaces and other public areas are another possibility for searching. You can discover what parks and open spaces exist in your area, together with the contact details of the responsible local council department, from your local library or tourist information office. This information can be found online at:

http://local.direct.gov.uk/LDGRedirect/index.jsp?LGSL=461&LGIL=8

In the early days of the hobby, in the UK, public areas were reckoned to be managed by custodians and reasonably accessible for metal detecting, as many still are in the USA. Following a British High Court ruling in the 1990s the local authority administering such areas was deemed to be the landowner and search permission needs to be obtained. A few enlightened councils do permit responsible metal detecting on public land and if your local council is among them, then find out what the rules are and you may have plenty of land to search. You may also gain permission by helping the park keeper or ranger find something. Bear in mind that some parks and pleasure gardens have closed down and the land may be accessible in some form or other.

If your local council bans metal detecting on their land, you may still be able to get permission but dealing with local government bureaucracy is fraught with difficulties and is not an experience for the faint hearted, so ensure, as best as you can, that the public places you want to search will be worth the effort. You will need to write to the council and you will stand a much better chance of succeeding if you can claim most or all of the following:

*You are carrying out a specific project, preferably in a defined area.

*You live and presumably pay council tax in the council's area.

*You have NCMD, or similar, public liability insurance.

*You have knowledge and/or evidence of the council consenting to activities on amenity grassland which is more harmful than metal detecting – games, sports, funfairs, bonfires, horse-riding, etc.

*You have knowledge and/or evidence of other members of the public taking issue with the council over activities in public open spaces.

You are unlikely to get a positive reply to your first letter. To win against officialdom you need to take the moral high-ground and keep responding with calm reasoned arguments and supporting evidence for your case. It might become a war of attrition but you stand a good chance of succeeding.

What are you paying your council tax for when they won't allow you to indulge in your harmless pastime? Why can anybody do almost anything else in the park without even asking? Why do they allow the funfair to drive huge trucks onto the park? Why do they allow the boy-scouts to have bonfires? If they say it's for charity, offer to give your decimal finds to charity. If they say they have a bylaw against metal detecting, ask for the documentation and the reason for the bylaw. The council can give exemptions from bylaws anyway: guide dogs for the blind are usually exempted from dog bylaws for instance.

If you are able to search on public land, leave your spade behind and only use small hand tools for finds extraction as a spade gives a very bad impression to the public who will undoubtedly be watching you. Use a polythene bag, drop-cloth or Frisbee to deposit the plug and excavated earth onto so you can put it all back in the hole without leaving a brown stain. Either avoid digging in dry weather or douse your filled holes with water. Also bear in mind that metal detectorists may have searched there before and most, if not all the easy targets, will already have been found. Your modern metal detector may go deeper than previous models used there but if you are not getting the finds, try the places which are more difficult to search, like under bushes.

Within parks, there are a number of features deserving attention:

*Bandstands, regularly used in the nineteenth and early twentieth centuries.

*Flower Beds, out of season or being prepared for planting.

*Drinking Fountains. About 80% of such fountains date back to Victorian times. On a hot summer's day, perhaps 100 people would visit for a drink and then relax in the surrounding grass area before continuing the journey. These surrounding areas are fantastic, the longer the fountain has been there, the greater the finds. If the fountain disappeared in the 1960s then the silver paper problem will be greatly reduced. Large scale maps of fifty years ago will show where fountains used to be, some parks had several fountains.

*Troughs where horses were watered can also be productive.

*Games pitches, search spectator areas only unless the actual pitch is undergoing maintenance.

*Gates, as entrance fees may have been charged for some events.

*Lidos or open-air swimming pools. The golden age of lidos in the United Kingdom was in the 1930s, when outdoor swimming became popular, and 169 were built across the UK as recreational facilities by local councils. Many lidos closed when foreign holidays became less expensive, but there has been a resurgence of interest in recent times and a number have been renovated and reopened. See: Janet Smith, Simon Inglis, *Liquid Assets: The Lidos and Open Air Swimming Pools of Britain,* (2005)

*Pathways especially those around the perimeter used by dog walkers and horse riders.

*Pavilions and other buildings.

*Playgrounds.

*Stalls may have been set up in some areas.

*Trees and bushes, which may have been used for shelter or shade, picnics, courting, etc.

Turf Mazes. Dating to around medieval times a turf maze is a labyrinth made by cutting a convoluted route through a level area of turf or lawn. Their purpose is open to conjecture. Some are located near religious houses and were said to be for crawling on hands and knees as a sort of pilgrimage to salvation, while others were used in May Day and similar celebrations. There are eight surviving in England, with names such as: Mizmaze, Troy Town, and Julian's Bower; all scheduled monuments and out of bounds to us, nevertheless it is estimated that there may once have been as many as 80–100 turf mazes in Britain. See: W.H. Matthews, *Mazes and Labyrinths,* (1922)

13 RECREATION

Amusement Parks evolved from three earlier traditions: travelling fairs, pleasure gardens, and expositions or exhibitions such as world fairs. The periodic fair of the Middle Ages, such as the Bartholomew Fair in England from 1133, was the earliest influence. By the eighteenth and nineteenth centuries, fairs had evolved into places of entertainment for the masses, where the public could view freak shows, acrobatics, conjuring and juggling, take part in competitions and walk through menageries.

Innovation in the 1860s and 1870s created mechanical rides, such as the steam-powered carousel notably from Frederick Savage of King's Lynn, Norfolk, whose fairground machinery was exported all over the world. The second influence was the pleasure garden. Fixed park amusement was further developed with the beginning of the world's fairs. The first world fair began in 1851 with the Crystal Palace in London. The purpose of the exposition was to celebrate the industrial achievement of the world's nations, while educating and entertaining visitors.

The first amusement park in Britain was Dreamland, Margate, opened in 1880; Blackpool Pleasure Beach followed in 1896. Thus began the era of the modern funfair ride, as the working classes were increasingly able to spend their disposable income on entertainment. Other parks opened in the early twentieth century and many have survived in one form or another. The later twentieth century has been a bit of a roller-coaster ride with some parks closing, some opening and some being destroyed by fire or the wrecking ball. As the industry is seasonal, it may be possible to gain permission to search going concerns out of season and closed venues at anytime. Bear in mind that some parks, like Blackpool, relocated so there may be scope to search former sites.

Bandstands. The first bandstands in Britain were built in the Royal Horticultural Society Gardens, South Kensington in 1861. Bandstands quickly became hugely popular and throngs of people would sit or stand around them enjoying the music. They were considered a necessity in parks and other open spaces by the end of the nineteenth century.

During World War II, iron fittings were removed from most bandstands to be recycled for the war effort. Many bandstands fell into disrepair and were boarded up in the late 1940s and 1950s as traditional recreational parks lost much of their appeal in favour of other attractions: such as cinema and television. Between 1979 and 2001, over half of the 438 bandstands in historic parks across the country were demolished, vandalized or disused. In the late 1990s the National Lottery and Heritage Lottery Fund invested a substantial sum in the restoration and rebuilding of over eighty bandstands across the country. Bandstands will be recorded on old large-scale Ordnance Survey maps.

Beauty spots. Modern day beauty spots are probably largely controlled by the National Trust, a Country Park or a Nature Reserve and while detecting in such places would not be impossible, gaining permission would not be easy. There are, however, numerous early beauty spots that have fallen out of favour for whatever reason. These are the ones to look out for in old guide books, newspapers and postcards.

Bicycling Sites. At the turn of the nineteenth century tens of thousands cycled out of cities and towns into the countryside. Contour Road Books provide routes and clues to resting spots.

Camping and Caravan sites. Recreational camping first became popular in Britain on the river Thames. By the 1880s large numbers took part in the pastime, which was connected to the late Victorian love of pleasure boating. The heavy early camping equipment was conveniently transported by boat, or craft that converted into tents were used. Thomas Hiram Holding, a British travelling tailor, popularised a different type of camping in the early twentieth century. He drew from his experience travelling across the American prairies with his parents and a later cycling and camping tour with friends in Ireland. His book, *Cycle and Camp in Connemara*, led to the formation of the first camping group in 1901, the Association of Cycle Campers. He wrote *The Camper's Handbook*, in 1908, sharing his enthusiasm for the great outdoors. There is a short list of camp sites in the back of the book.

Cunningham's camp, near Douglas, Isle of Man, opened 1894, was probably the world's first commercial camp site. In 1906, the Association of Cycle Campers, boasting several hundred members, opened its first camp site, in Weybridge, Surrey. In 1910 the Association was merged into the

National Camping Club. World War I curtailed camping activity, but the renamed Camping Club of Great Britain and Ireland enjoyed a revival, in 1919, when Sir Robert Baden-Powell (of Boy Scouts fame) became its president.

By the 1960s camping had become well established for family holidays, appealing to many classes of society and numerous camp sites are to be found across Europe and North America. Caravanning increasingly became popular alongside camping, which was reflected in the organisation becoming The Camping and Caravanning Club, in 1983. Recent developments include Glamping (glamorous camping) combining camping with the luxury and facilities of a hotel. You will find a comprehensive directory of British camp sites here:

https://www.ukcampsite.co.uk/index.asp

There are of course many static caravan sites which could also be productively searched. https://www.caravansitefinder.co.uk/

The camp sites I have searched have all been productive. At tent sites things are easily lost and on static caravan sites items are lost in between the caravans. Ask for permission during the winter months when the site is little used and your ground disturbance heals better. There are some sites here known to allow metal detecting:

http://www.campsitechatter.com/specialisms/campsites-for-detectorists/campsites-allowing-metal-detecting#.YPFJiJhKiUk

Carnival sites. Carnival is traditionally a Western Christian festive season that occurs before Lent. The main events typically occurred during February or early March, during Shrovetide (or Pre-Lent). Carnival typically involves public celebrations, including events such as parades, public street parties and other entertainments, combining some elements of a circus. In Britain today apart from a few of this type of lavish event, such as Notting Hill Carnival, most carnivals involve local groups and businesses dressing-up vehicle propelled floats and participants, together with bands, etc. which form a procession through the streets collecting money for charity. Nevertheless some carnivals have existed for hundreds of years. While there may be some prospects for streetcombing immediately after the event the best sport would be at mustering points at the start and end of the procession and any grassed areas along the route. The carnival may have used the same places and routes for many years while earlier routes could be found from old local newspapers.

Circus grounds. In Ancient Rome, the circus was an exhibition building for horse and chariot races, equestrian shows, mock battles, gladiatorial combat, and trained animal displays. They were based on the ancient Greek hippodromes, for horse racing. Roman circus buildings were effectively oval in shape. After the fall of Rome, large circus buildings fell out of use and itinerant performers, travelled between towns throughout Europe, performing at local fairs. In 1768, Philip Astley, the father of the modern circus, set up a ring, performing exhibitions of trick horse riding in an open field called Ha'Penny Hatch on the south side of the River Thames. In 1770, Astley hired acrobats, clowns, jugglers and tightrope walkers to fill in the pauses between acts. Circuses were often held in purpose-built buildings in large cities, such as the London Hippodrome. The Royal Circus was opened in London in 1782 followed by many other permanent circuses in cities throughout Europe.

The earliest modern circuses were performed in open-air structures with limited covered seating. From the late eighteenth to late nineteenth century, custom-made circus buildings (often wooden) were built with various types of seating, a centre ring, and sometimes a stage. The traditional large tents commonly known as "big tops" were introduced from 1826 as touring circuses superseded static venues. For the last 200 years or so, most areas in Britain have had annual or perhaps more frequent visits from the circus. The circus ground is sometimes waste land, sometimes parkland, heath or common and often a farmer's field on the outskirts of town or village. Depending on the land use the site may vary from year to year and may have been held in a dozen different fields, all worth searching. Finding aids include newspapers, old photos and postcards, and council records.

Fairgrounds. The trading fairs of earlier times (see chapter 17, Trading) were in decline by the nineteenth century and were gradually taken over by entertainments such as shows and rides. By the end of the nineteenth century 200 fairs were held in Britain every weekend from Easter until November and that has continued through until today, save for the war years. Clearly you will not find much where fairs are held on hard surfaces but many were, or are, held on grass and other soft surfaces, where a goodly portion of the large amount of money changing hands will be trodden into the ground. You can discover some of these sites through local newspapers, local histories, postcards and talking to senior citizens.

Festivals and concerts. Large-scale outdoor modern music festivals began in the 1960s; one of the most famous being the Isle of Wight Festival which attracted over 500,000 attendees in 1970. The Reading Festival began as the National Jazz and Blues Festival in the 1960s and the first Glastonbury Festival was held in 1970. In the twenty-first century the number of festivals has grown significantly. In 2020 the number of UK music festivals was approximately 240.

https://en.wikipedia.org/wiki/List_of_music_festivals_in_the_United_Kingdom Other festivals include food, books, history and crafts: https://en.wikipedia.org/wiki/List_of_festivals_in_the_United_Kingdom

Garden Fetes. These fetes were a one day event at a manor house village green, inn, vicarage, rectory, or nearest grass field to a church. Originally they were a harvest festival celebration but became a general fund-raiser for churches of any denomination. Many were advertised in local newspapers or will be remembered by older citizens.

Holiday accommodation. Providing your partner is OK with it, when staying at bed and breakfast, farms, cottages, etc. it is always worth asking the owner of if you can detect on any land they have. There are also a number of closed holiday camps such as Hemsby Holiday Park in Norfolk. Another option is metal detecting holidays:

https://www.metaldetectingholidays.com/what-we-offer

Maypoles. A maypole is a tall wooden pole erected as a part of various European folk festivals, which usually occur on May 1st or Pentecost (Whitsun) but can take place in Midsummer (June 20-26). The maypole can be a permanent fixture or erected specifically for a festival, often on village greens, before being taken down again.

The maypole's origin stems from pagan worship in Iron Age and early Medieval cultures surviving to the present day as folk tradition. Festivals generally involve dancing around the maypole and the usual merriment. Sites of maypoles can be found from old photographs and postcards, local knowledge, pub names, newspapers, etc.

Medieval Tournament Sites. Despite the Hollywood image, most knights in the Age of Chivalry were violent men, whose lives revolved around hunting, war and tournaments.

Tournaments or tourneys originated in France around the tenth century and were imported into England with the Normans as 'French Combat'. They continued to the sixteenth century although several attempts to shut them down were made by several kings and the Church. The first tournaments were mock battles or melees between two groups of mounted knights, numbering up to 200 combatants. The two heavily armed groups would charge at each other and not surprisingly, there were many deaths and serious injuries.

The events became more civilised over time, with blunted weapons and smaller scale melees, which were slowly replaced by jousts between two knights at a time. Tournaments were enormously expensive so only kings and the richest nobles could afford to hold them and they became an extravagant extension of great court occasions. Of course the knights had a large entourage of assistants: armourers, farriers, grooms, harness-makers, ostlers, saddlers and squires and the event would be thronged with spectators. The local accommodation would be overflowing and the surrounding fields covered with hundreds of tents. Grandstands were erected for the ladies, and everywhere people, including whores and cutpurses, would be making merry.

The major tournament sites were in North-East France and if you can track down a tournament site you will certainly make great finds. Five sites were licensed in Britain by Richard I, though undoubtedly many more existed before and since. Raker Field in Blyth, Nottinghamshire, is believed to be one tournament site. In medieval times Blyth was of great importance and had a market and fair. Brackley, was one of several tournament sites in Northamptonshire, held on the open space known as Bayards or Bear's Green. A Tudor tilting ground is preserved in Gawsworth Hall in Cheshire. Dunstable seems to be the most mentioned tournament site and there is also Langwith Common near York. The coming of firearms put and end to traditional tournaments and many former tournament sites became horse racing tracks.

Motor Touring Sites Before WWII car ownership was the preserve of the wealthier members of society and consequently discovering places they motored to for recreation will likely hold valuable losses. Almost all the places visited by weekend motorists in the 1920s and 1930s were described in newspapers (particularly Thursday and Friday editions) and magazines of the time. A well known motoring correspondent of the period was A S Jenkinson who wrote for the *London Evening News*, among others. The British Newspaper Archive has digitised thousands of pages of newspapers and magazines which can be searched online. Old guide books such as Ward Lock red guides cater for motoring trips and old handbooks of the AA and RAC could also be consulted.

Mount Pleasants were natural or artificial mounds used as playgrounds exclusively by wealthy eighteenth century aristocracy who left good quality coins and jewellery behind. There are over 100 Mount Pleasant place-names in the UK.

Picnic areas. From the eighteenth century, estate owners held lavish picnics on their estates, generally near the house. Many estates were effectively dissolved in the twentieth century so there may be opportunities on former estate land. Of course there will have been smaller affairs which may have been held some distance from the house; a silver monogrammed spoon turned up half-a-mile away from its base for instance. As leisure time increased, the masses took to picnicking, taking meals to local beauty spots and outdoor events. Many popular picnic areas now are country parks or National Trust properties. A good number have also been forgotten but may be found from local guides, such as Ward Locks red guides, ramblers and walkers guides, Railway guides (Bradshaw's), etc.

Pleasure gardens. Most, if not all, manor houses had a pleasure garden but there were public pleasure gardens in London and around other cities and towns. Vauxhall Gardens, London, founded in 1661 was one of the first pleasure gardens. By the late eighteenth century, the site had an admission fee for its many attractions. It regularly drew enormous crowds, with its paths often noted for romantic assignations; tightrope walkers, hot air balloon ascents, concerts and fireworks providing amusement. Although the gardens were originally designed for the elite, they soon attracted all classes of society. Public firework displays were put on at Marylebone Gardens, and Cremorne Gardens offered music, dancing, and animal acrobatics displays. There were several other pleasure gardens in London, while outside notably there was Belle Vue Gardens in Manchester and Rosherville Gardens at Gravesend. There must have been many others around the country. The majority of these gardens have closed or contracted but any vestiges that can be found will undoubtedly turn up some good finds.

St Helena Gardens, Rotherhithe

Rallies and Commercial. Several metal detecting rallies are held in the UK every year where you can buy a ticket, turn up and detect. You will find these advertised in metal detecting magazines. What you may find is very much a lottery but good finds and prizes do turn up. I won a metal detector in a token hunt on one rally and on another I found a George III gold sovereign. There are also a few commercial farms where you can pay a fee for a day's detecting, these tend to come and go as the fields become less productive over time, even with regular ploughing. Nevertheless, no field is ever exhausted of finds. One such farm is here:

https://www.airgunfarm.co.uk/essex-metal-detecting

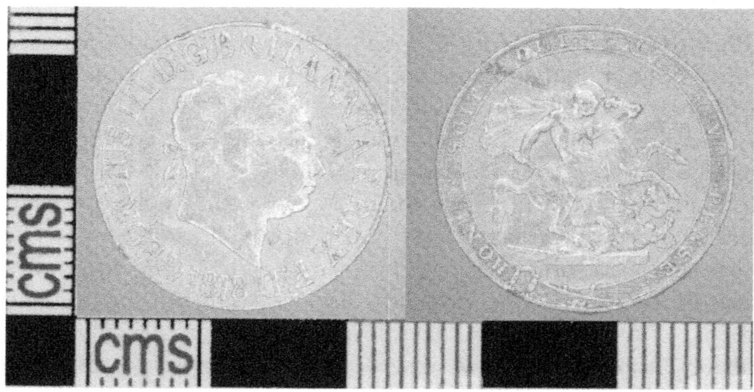

George III Sovereign

South-facing slopes are warmed by the sun more than those facing any other direction and as such many have attracted occupation, good farming, picnickers and a place to rest for passers-by. If there is an interesting view from the slope, so much the better.

Spas. A spa is a location where mineral-rich spring water, or seawater, is used to give medicinal baths. Mineral waters were believed to cure ailments in prehistoric times. The Romans built abundant large and complex baths throughout the Empire. The Roman bath became a focus for social and recreational activity. With the decline of the Roman Empire, public baths often became places of promiscuous behaviour, and spread diseases. Medieval church authorities endeavoured to close down public baths, which went into decline.

People still sought out hot and cold springs, or holy wells, to cure various ailments. In an age of religious fervour, the benefits of the water were attributed to God or one of the saints. In 1326, Collin le Loup, an iron-master from Liège, Belgium, discovered the chalybeate (iron-bearing) springs of Spa, Belgium, which developed into a renowned health resort. The name "spa" became synonymous with any health resort located beside natural springs. In sixteenth-century England, medicinal bathing was revived at towns like Bath and in 1596 William Slingsby discovered a chalybeate spring at Harrogate, Yorkshire. He built an enclosed well at what became the first resort in England for drinking medicinal waters, then Dr. Timothy Bright discovered a second well and called the resort: The English Spa.

In Scarborough, Yorkshire, in 1626, Elizabeth Farrow discovered a stream of acidic water issuing from one of the cliffs deemed to have beneficial health properties and founded Scarborough Spa. Visitors flocked to the town, sea bathing was added to the cure, and Scarborough became Britain's first seaside resort.

Most upper-class Europeans washed their clothes with water frequently and washed only their faces, in the early seventeenth century. They felt that bathing the entire body was a lower-class activity; but the upper-class slowly began changing their attitudes toward bathing as a way to restore health. The wealthy drank and bathed in the waters at health resorts in great numbers. In 1702, Queen Anne, bathed at Bath and shortly after the country spa was transformed into the English social capital. Bath set the standard for other spas in Europe to follow. The wealthy and worthies arrived on a seasonal basis, ostensibly to bathe and drink the water; they also came to display their opulence. Social activities at Bath included dances, concerts, playing cards, lectures, and promenading down the street. Similar activities occurred in health resorts throughout Europe. Various social and economic classes, aristocrats, prosperous farmers or retired military men selected specific seasons during the year, staying between one and several months vacation at each resort.

During the eighteenth century, a revival in the medical uses of spring water was promoted by enlightened physicians across Europe. This revival changed the way of taking a spa treatment from individuals drinking prescribed dosages alone in their room, to taking exercise before drinking at the spring. This increased the medicinal benefits obtained and gradually physical activity became part of the European bathing regime.

In the nineteenth century, bathing became a more accepted practice as physicians realized some of the benefits that cleanliness could provide ultimately leading to The Baths and Wash-houses Acts, 1846-1896. This resulted in increased facilities for bathing and washing clothes, and more people participating. In England, hot showers were installed in barracks and schools by the 1880s. Enormous bathhouses came later in the nineteenth century as a renewed preference for an elaborate bathing ritual to cure ills and improve health came into vogue. Formal garden spaces were laid out in their resorts, and the tour books always mentioned the roomy, woodsy offerings in the vicinity and the faster-paced evening diversions.

European spas provided additional facilities for guests, including dancing, fishing, gambling, golf, horse racing, horse riding, hunting, sight-seeing, skating, tennis, and theatre.

Many popular sites in towns and cities have been lost to development but look for minor rural spas and their neighbouring hilltops and beauty spots, commons and bridleways within 10 miles of spa. Try *B. BRADSHAW'S DICTIONARY OF BATHING PLACES, CLIMATIC HEALTH RESORTS, MINERAL WATERS, SEA BATHS, AND HYDROPATHIC ESTABLISHMENTS. Giving the names of Doctors; Hotels which can be recommended with confidence; and other useful information. WITH A MAP SHEWING THE STATIONS NAMED, AND AN ITINERARY OF THE QUICKEST AND CHEAPEST ROUTES BY RAIL, BOATS, CARRIAGES, etc., AND SEVERAL SMALLER MAPS AND PLANS.* (London, 1898)

Traditional Events. There is a tradition in a small Kent village of the lord of the manor setting up a running race, in 1638, between young men and young maidens, for a monetary prize. This race took place twice annually among a great concourse of the neighbouring gentry and inhabitants and endured well into the nineteenth century. I was able to search two of the, at least, three sites associated with this race and came away with bags full of coins and personal items. I am sure this wasn't the only race of its type in the country. There are upwards of 40 cheese rolling races held annually in Britain, with a long history and a number of other events:
https://www.britainexpress.com/what's_new/calendar_of_events.htm

Viewpoints. Modern Ordnance Survey Landranger and Explorer maps, mark viewpoints, many of which have probably been used for centuries for defence, picnics and just to enjoy the view. Similarly, also shown are triangulation pillars erected on high ground for surveying the land, which would also attract the public for the view and picnics. There were many, mainly coastal, lookout sites manned by the coastguard or their predecessors and these too would be worth exploring and can be found from older maps.

Village Halls. England alone boasts 10,000 village halls, most of which are community owned; many also have open land or sports fields attached. There is clearly much coming and going which will have also gone on in the past. Any open land you can get access to will repay searching.

14 ROUTES

History can be seen in roads and tracks as much as in towns and villages. The routes joining settlements were vitally important and their usage over the centuries may be reflected in a wealth of finds. Although today's population is much larger than in our ancestors' day, you only need to transpose the number of vehicles on the roads into a similar proportion of travellers over the centuries, to realise how important routes of communication are to everyday life. Before the coming of the bicycle and internal combustion engine most people walked. There were relatively few horses, carts and carriages. The amount of use roads and track ways had in the past are directly related to the losses we can expect to find.

Roads carried traffic for trade and commerce: from drovers, carters and packhorses, to lords and ladies, highwaymen, tinkers and tramps; friends visiting each other, soldiers policing the country or marching to war, funeral processions, churchgoers and harvesting bands, all of them are represented by metal objects that they have dropped, lying buried in the earth. Many of these artefacts will simply have been lost, but others may now lie where they do as the result of falls or accidents; a rearing horse or a stumble into a waterlogged pothole, while others are the remnants from an attack by cutpurses or highwaymen.

Bridleways, Footpaths and Public Rights of Way are usually owned by the landowner of the land, over which the path or way crosses. Where the way is fenced off from surrounding land the relevant highway authority, local authority or National Park often owns it and that would usually include roadside verges. The highway authority also has a statutory duty to keep all rights of way open and will certainly talk to the landowner if they receive complaints that your activities are in any way interfering with anyone's rights of free passage, so be careful!

Ancient track ways. The forerunners of our modern road-system began in prehistoric times. When farmers settled in the Neolithic period they needed paths between farm and pasture, and between farms and tribal meeting places. By the Early Bronze Age, around 3000 BC, the first long-distance tracks came into existence, running along the treeless hills and downs of Britain, and had fully developed by the Iron Age.

There were four major prehistoric ways:

*The 'Harrow Way' from Seaton, Devon to Dover, Kent.

*The 'Icknield Way' from Norfolk to Wiltshire.

*The 'Ridgeway' which runs from the Wash to the Dorset coast.

*The 'Jurassic Way', which runs from Stamford, Lincolnshire to Banbury, Oxfordshire.

These track ways joined important prehistoric sites to known Neolithic flint mines and surface iron deposits particularly in Oxfordshire and Northamptonshire. The track ways tended to run on high ground but below the hilltops and tree line. Secondary parallel tracks often developed to avoid ruts and bad ground. Some of these ways and their alternative routes were re-engineered by the Romans, others remain as forgotten 'green ways', but the majority, survive as usable paths, especially where they have been incorporated into long-distance footpaths. They are well worth following and, where not accessible for metal detecting, surrounding land will undoubtedly yield exciting finds.

Cracks in paving. Coins and jewellery can easily find its way into cracks in paving (or floorboards). Old paving like church paths would be well worth searching, with permission of course.

Crossroads, or paths, or where several routes meet may be a market or settlement site. From the early days of Christianity up until 1823 it was customary to bury suicides in a shallow grave by the roadside and particularly at or near crossroads. It is unlikely that anyone would have dared to rifle such unhallowed corpses for their possessions, which may be lying in the vicinity. Hoards too were popularly buried nearby using the crossroads as a marker. Areas where old tracks cross boundaries are also worth investigating.

Country Lanes may have been used by travellers, pedlars, chapmen, pack animals, ox carts, horse and horse-drawn transport for centuries; straight sections of track may be Roman or earlier. Pick out long stretches from maps, which may not be continuous now but may be marked by boundaries.

Any lane leading in a fairly direct line from one parish church to another would be well used. Lanes which lead from and to fords on major rivers also. Where fords are close to or on routes to cathedral towns or religious shrines search carefully around fords and lanes for pilgrim badges.

Drovers' Roads. A drovers' road, driftway, drove [road] or droveway is a route for driving livestock on the hoof from one place to another, such as to market. Many drovers' roads were ancient routes of unknown age; others date to medieval or more recent times.

Some of the best medieval finds have been found on ancient routes and track ways used several hundred years ago by packhorse teams and drovers. There are countless miles of once busy routes, especially in moorland areas, now readily accessible via public paths and bridleways.

As cities and towns increased in size during the later medieval period it became necessary to supply these populations with fresh meat, which was accomplished by driving animals from cattle rearing Wales, Ireland and Scotland, south to the southern English fairs, grazing and fattening grounds. Sheep, geese and turkeys were also driven. Industry too, made use of routes to carry goods by packhorse, from factory to market, up until the eighteenth century when turnpike roads, canals and railways took the traffic.

Drovers' roads are often wider than other roads, able to accommodate large herds or flocks. Packhorse ways were quite narrow as the horses moved in single file, whereas drove roads were at least 40 feet (12 m) and up to 90 feet (27 m) across with wide grazing verges on either side, known as the "long acre".

Where many original drovers' roads have been converted into single carriageway metalled roads, unusually wide verges often give an indication of the road's origin. In Wales, the start of many drovers' roads are often recognisable by being deeply set into the countryside, with high earth walls or hedges. The most characteristic feature of these roads is the occasional sharp turn in the road, which provided cover for animals and men in severe rain or snow. Some drovers' roads crossed mountains.

Drovers (those droving or driving livestock) accompanied their livestock either on foot or on horseback, travelling substantial distances. Rural England, Wales and Scotland are crossed by numerous drove roads that were used for this trade, many of which are now no more than tracks, and some lost altogether. The word "drover" (porthmon in Welsh) is used for those engaged in long distance trade: distances which could cover much of the length of Britain while "cattle driver" was used for those taking cattle to local markets.

It wasn't quite *Rawhide,* as some of you will remember the TV series, but controlling herds of three or four hundred animals on narrow roads, keeping them healthy, and feeding them en route, over several weeks or months, required expertise and authority.

Some form of drovers' roads existed in Romano-British times and certainly throughout the Early Middle Ages. Many lengths of the Welsh Road through the English Midlands coincide with manorial or parish boundaries, suggesting that they predate them and probably had pre-Roman origins as an ancient track way.

In Great Britain, *Drove* as a place name can be traced to the early thirteenth century, and there are records of cattle driven from Wales to London and sheep from Lincolnshire to York in the early fourteenth century. Drovers from Scotland were licensed in 1359 to drive stock through England. These may be simply the earliest records of a more ancient trade. There is increasing evidence for large-scale cattle-rearing in Bronze Age and Iron Age Britain. Cattle and sheep were part of the Romano-British economy. By the Anglo-Saxon period there was long distance movement of cattle.

What is certain is that during the medieval period there was a substantial trade in cattle out of Wales into England, to which cattle from Ireland were added. These were driven across Somerset, Wiltshire and Berkshire to feed the growing population of London. The drovers made use of ancient ridgeways, including the Ridgeway over the Berkshire Downs, the Old Shaftesbury Drove and the Ox Drove leading from Shaftesbury and Blandford to Salisbury. There were also short droves between London and the Home Counties for fattening stock out in rural areas then taking them back to the city. This would also have occurred around other cities and towns. Places named Little London are sites of cattle markets and names related to Wales, Scotland and Ireland, usually mark drovers routes.

Concentrate searches in open areas where routes are still accessible. Study Ordnance Survey maps to pick out footpaths. A small clump of Scots pines were often planted as stopping-place markers. Look out for old inns called drovers, packhorse or black bull. Drovers may have camped and merchants often rode out to meet the drovers and buy livestock before they got to market, particularly at nearby tollhouses, where keepers let out land. Cattle needed to be watered twice daily. A watercourse was the best solution as the animals could spread out providing there were no steep banks. The drovers travelled at around two miles per hour, depending on terrain and up to 12 hours per day. So expect camps around 10-20 miles apart. The remains of campsites can be identified by football sized stones for tents, fireplaces, pot boilers, corrals and grazing land, ponds and watering places. Patches of deep green grass caused by regular manuring are a sure sign of grazing. A night's grazing cost a halfpenny which remains today as a place, route or field name.

Green Lanes. Various attempts to provide a map of ancient track ways have been made, such as Hippisley Cox, *The Green Roads of England,* (1914). It was not until the turnpike roads of the early eighteenth century that new roads were built to match the Roman communication system, 1300 years earlier. Many of the early roads still exist, such as the ridgeways, holloways, dykes, tracks, Roman roads and streets, saltways and drove roads. The contraction of villages, migrations of populations to towns and industry, and historical events have often hidden Britain's ancient roads or stranded them as 'green lanes' dotted throughout our countryside. All it takes to rediscover an 'old road' near you is a little imagination, some research, a keen eye for clues still hidden in the countryside and a bit of trouble to find them.

Lay-bys. Vehicle parking areas at the roadside are generally hard surfaced but usually have a soft surface behind. There is lots of activity in these places with opportunities for losses: picnics, vehicle maintenance, catering, flower, fruit and vegetable stands, etc.

Ley Lines. Alfred Watkins in *The Old Straight Track,* (1925) suggests that ancient track ways can be traced by lining up various ancient features such as barrows, mounds, standing stones, cairns and churches, which he called ley lines. Watkins' contention was that prehistoric man had built structures on straight tracks so you only have to find the ley line having at least three points and it will reveal the ancient track. There has been much controversy over the theory, particularly that with so many ancient features in the landscape, some are bound to line-up; features on the same ley line differ in age (but ancient sites tend to get re-used) and Watkin's ruler wasn't as straight as he would have us believe. A whole modern folklore has also developed giving ley lines an unintended paranormal or even extraterrestrial meaning. Nevertheless Watkins makes a compelling argument that prehistoric man was perfectly capable of laying out a network of straight tracks that the Romans found and improved upon when the legions invaded Britain in 43 AD. Many hoards have been found around ley lines.

Lover's Lanes. Dating from 1853, a lovers' lane is a secluded area where people engage in romantic or sexual activity. While they would originally have been lanes, today they are more likely to be car parks in secluded rural areas. The seclusion sometimes leads to crime, which may add to the losses. Dogging is probably a more recent development.

Milestones were used by the Romans on their roads although only around 117 remain in situ today. It should be possible to estimate roughly where they would have been placed on main Roman routes at one Roman mile intervals (1481 metres, 1618 yards). Milestones largely fell out of use until the seventeenth century when parishes were legally required to erect them at crossroads and on the moors. Turnpike Trusts too were required to erect them on their turnpike roads. Around 9000 survive on some 20,000 miles of road which had them. Many of the survivors are old and decayed, others like new, they stretch throughout the UK. Countless numbers have disappeared but their sites are recorded on old maps. Apart from coins lost while they were being used as a seat, or left by tramps for other tramps passing that way, they are a possible site for hoards. For details of recorded milestones see:

https://www.milestonesociety.co.uk/databases-information/

Packhorse routes. Although Roman roads were built to last they were not generally maintained once the Romans left and wheeled transport became difficult to impossible to use. Packhorses, which also include mules, donkeys and ponies, were heavily used to transport goods and minerals in England from medieval times until the first turnpike roads and canals were built in the eighteenth century. Many routes crossed the Pennines between Lancashire and Yorkshire, enabling the transport of cloth, coal, fleeces, limestone, and salt. Some routes were named for their use or structure, such as Limersgate ("gate" is a road or way) and the Long Causeway; others after landmarks. Wayside crosses along the routes marked medieval paths.

Most packhorses were small, stocky horses named Galloways, from the area where they were originally bred. Each horse could carry about 240 pounds (110 kg) in weight, spread between two panniers. Typically a packhorse train would number between 12 and 20, travelling in single file. They averaged about 25 miles (40 km) a day. About 1000 packhorses a day passed through Clitheroe before 1750.

As the need for cross-Pennine transportation increased, the main routes were improved, often by laying stone setts parallel to the horse track to facilitate wheeled transport.

The canals and metalled roads of the eighteenth century made the ancient packhorse routes largely obsolete although their use continued into the nineteenth century on paths across wilderness areas called packhorse routes, roads or trails. Look out for distinctive narrow, low-sided, stone, arched packhorse bridges. The Packhorse is a common public house name throughout England and may signify local routes or overnight stops.

Paths and tracks. Any footpath or track, regardless of length is a potential treasure trail, which only needs a little research for great returns. If a footpath is used by seven people daily then in 100 years it would have seen over 250,000 journeys. If one person in a 1000 dropped a metal object, notwithstanding that some will have been recovered, then there is likely to be over 200 objects buried on the path. All tracks are, or were, there for a reason; people use or used them. So even if they do not go anywhere today, they are worth investigating.

From modern and older maps establish the original route and possible purpose, mark all potential loss features, such as changes of level, mud patches, gates, stiles, resting places, views and fords; search these areas carefully. Many coin hoards have been found close to footpaths. Hoards were buried for safekeeping just outside habitation. Note the point from which a traveller would have sighted the settlement and look for a place of concealment; often a wooded area for easy digging and natural landmark.

Search three times the apparent with of the path or track to allow for people wandering and, on arable land, the route wandering as it is ploughed and reinstated.

Pavement grass verges. Objects dropped on pavements, will often find their way onto grass verges, be obscured and end up becoming buried.

Pilgrim routes. A few fortunate searchers have already found pilgrim relics, mainly on the tidal riverbanks of the Thames and Medway, which were crossed by thousands of pilgrims travelling to the shrine of Thomas-a-Becket at Canterbury. There were at least thirty other pilgrims' shrines in Medieval England, not including those to which Scottish and Welsh travellers made equally long journeys. The areas around these sites and the routes which led to them often have substantial numbers of lost or discarded badges alongside the numerous hammered silver coins that were dropped along the way.

These other important shrines were: Beverley, Bromholm, Crowland, Durham, Ely, Glastonbury, Gloucester, Hailes, Hereford, Hexham, Jarrow, Kings Lynn, Lastingham, Lichfield, Lincoln, Lindisfarne, Malmesbury, Norwich, Repton, Ripon, St Albans, Salisbury, Shaftesbury, Walsingham, Whitby, Winchester, Whitchurch, Worcester and York.

Likely hunting grounds for pilgrims' losses include routes leading directly to the shrine. Search:

*All old lanes, green roads and public footpaths.

*Abbeys, churches & other religious buildings on the route to the shrine. Pilgrims badges were probably sold there.

*Medieval bridges. Monks often sold badges from booths on the bridge.

*The shrine. If accessible, the land around will be rich in medieval losses.

*Hamlets and villages one (or more) day's travelling (on foot) from the shrine. Look for sites of ancient inns.

*Holy wells. Pilgrims probably bought ampullae there.

*Fords. Many badges and other items lost during crossings. Search banks and riverbeds.

In the medieval period the shrines were often surrounded by monks selling all manner of souvenirs including silver bells, necklaces for holding ampullae containing holy water, rosary beads and pins, not to mention badges. Such ground must certainly pay dividends, but if the site of the shrine is inaccessible you will have to look further afield. As pilgrims walked or rode to the shrines, the routes they followed can be traced. Identify the oldest roads, tracks, and footpaths leading by fairly direct routes to the shrine. Wherever these routes take in religious buildings or villages spaced at roughly a day's, or multiple of days', travelling time from the shrine you have a spot likely to hold losses.

Your chance of good finds will be even better if the route crosses water. All ancient fords, bridges and holy wells will be worth searching and some may now have disappeared. Their locations can be found either by place-name research or by looking at very old maps.

Roadside verges and embankments may be the remains of paths and tracks before they were metalled and would be worth searching particularly if the road is old. Works on road verges can often bring up lost objects. Check out where possible, with permission from the site manager, trenches, spoil heaps, etc. There may be Health & Safety issues but you may be allowed to search out of working hours. Wear long sleeved Hi-vis on roadsides and any other safety gear required.

Roman roads. The best way to locate potentially productive sites for Roman coins and artefacts is to study the Roman communication system. The Romans constructed over 10,000 miles of all-weather roads in Britain as well as using and improving existing navigable rivers. Good roads were important to facilitate the rapid movement of troops; to supply the forts and support the towns and villa estates. To keep roads as short as possible, they were laid in a straight line of sight, using existing tracks where possible, unless obstructions or extreme gradients dictated otherwise. If direction varied it was usually slight and only at high points where the surveyors took a new line of sight. Roads needed to be passable throughout the year so they had to withstand the British climate. To prevent erosion, roads were cambered so water would run off into ditches dug along both sides. Road surfaces comprised stone-paving or compacted dirt or gravel according to the perceived amount of use and importance.

Roman road near Bainbridge, Yorkshire. Copyright Chris Gunns and licensed for reuse under a Creative Commons Licence

All Roman buildings, where people lived, worked and played had access to a road or river or both. Towns and smaller settlements were usually built straddling or at the side of roads, often at a crossroads or where a road crossed a river. Forts, typically a day's march apart, will be found along roads, interspersed with inns to serve the need of travellers and messengers. The advice of Roman writer Cato was to build villas away from and out of sight of the road for security, hence they are not normally found at the roadside. Villas will be located within easy reach of towns and may be built little more than a mile apart in the South East. In essence, all Roman roads lead to finds. You can use maps and aerial photography to find not only the roads themselves but forts, settlements, inns, villas and other buildings that are guaranteed to produce Roman metalwork.

The Ordnance Survey (OS) map of Roman Britain, which has been produced in six editions since 1924, gives an excellent overview. While I advocate having the most recent edition with up to date information, I prefer the 1956 third edition particularly for its wealth of Roman smaller finds missing from later maps. The potential for finding sites from these maps is tremendous as they not only show known features but give tantalising clues to those yet to be found.

The Ordnance Survey historical map is not the only worthy source of information. The late Ivan D Margary, Britain's foremost expert on Roman roads, wrote *Roman Ways in the Weald*, (1948 & later revisions) and *Roman Roads in Britain*, (1955, 2 vols, North and South divided at the Fosse Way/Bristol Channel; (1973 revision is a single volume)). Although there has been much written on British Roman roads since, these are still the most comprehensive studies.

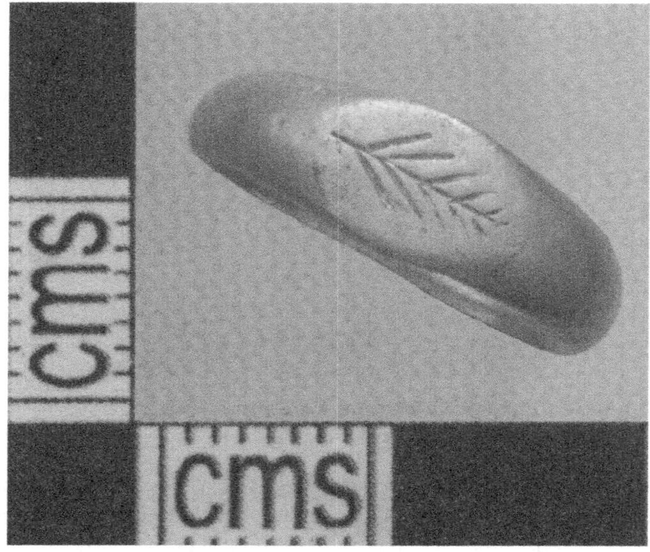

Roman gold ring found alongside road

Salt Ways were developed for moving salt and may have followed earlier routes. The salt way from Droitwich and the Cheshire Salt 'wiches' runs down through the West Midlands to Princes Risborough. Trains of pack horses belonging to the salters proceeded south to the cities, carrying the great quantities of salt required to preserve the fish and meat needed in every household during the winter. Radiating from the brine-pans of Droitwich, in particular, salt ways and saltergates cover the country. Of special interest are the open spaces by bridges and fords where the salters would make temporary camp. Names such as 'Salters Bridge', 'Salters Hill' and 'Sal(t)ford' suggest recognised places en-route. It is worth exploring these lanes.

Steps and stairways for mounting horses or carriages invite objects to be dropped around them.

Stiles. Most of Britain was open land up until the seventeenth century. Villagers had plots of land, to farm, distributed between large fields of available arable land. It was an inefficient system that was replaced by redistributing land into approx 10 acres per landholder and necessitated enclosure which followed in the eighteenth century, mainly ending grazing rights. Small farmers lost their land and large estates became larger. The landscaping of manorial parks and changes in agriculture necessitated fences, hedges and walls to keep animals in or out of fields but there was a massive introduction of stiles to facilitate people moving around the landscape. Negotiating of stiles is bound to cause a few losses of metallic items and whether used today or not, will repay searching around.

Turnpikes and tollbars. During the Roman period roads were developed mainly to facilitate movement of troops and stores; they also serviced the towns. The Romans used slaves to repair and maintain the roads. After the Romans left, the Anglo-Saxons, had little use for them, being basically farmers trading locally and roads deteriorated into a route or right of way between one place and another rather than a distinct highway. The almost total lack of hedges and fences in medieval times encouraged detours over adjacent land, if a road became impassable. In the thirteenth century the king attempted to stem the decline by introducing various acts and statutes. Lords of manors were required to employ men to fell trees and cut back undergrowth up to 200 ft on any highway between market towns once annually and fill large holes and ruts. Look for roads between market towns with wide verges although many will have been encroached over the years.

The acts led to further decline as many could not afford the additional expense. This situation went on for a further 250 years, until in 1555 the first Highways Act successfully imposed State control of the roads by making parishes responsible. The first turnpike trust was set up in 1706 and eventually there were almost eleven hundred trusts, covering over 2300 miles of roads. The aim was to collect tolls which would pay for the upkeep and repair of the roads. Typical rates were one penny for a horse, sixpence for wheeled transport and a halfpenny per head of cattle. The military and locals passed free.

The term turnpike was derived from the pikestaff placed across the road as a barrier, which was turned to allow traffic to pass. Important routes had toll houses where the keeper lived, while on lesser routes the keeper may have had to make do with a tent or hollow tree. Good bonuses, exceeding what they would get from bribery, were paid to keepers who collected the highest amounts of tolls. Many toll houses were cleverly designed octagonal buildings and usually sited at the junction between two roads. This enabled the keeper to see in all directions. Some of the bigger toll houses had tunnels from inside the house to the opposite side of the roads. Keepers often had land which they rented for stabling and camping for the travellers.

There are many hundreds of toll sites around the country which are well worth searching and especially the field immediately before the toll. There is a comprehensive listing of turnpikes and tollbars here:

http://www.turnpikes.org.uk/

15 SERVICES

Many services will be on hard-standing and only searchable eyes only, but check any soft ground nearby where coins may have rolled or migrated. Check return draws on coin-operated services. Most services will only require a short time to search so perhaps select a number of candidates in a small area, which can be checked in a morning or afternoon.

Bus stops. Impatient travellers would drop the change they had painstakingly sorted out, particularly with the introduction of pay as you enter buses. Disembarking passengers could also drop things, stepping off the bus. I once found a gold ankle-chain at a bus stop.

Car Parks. Sand, grass, gravel and other soft-surfaced parking areas are well-worth searching for mainly modern objects, but you never know what may have been lost there before the invention of the automobile. While fumbling for keys in the evening a driver might easily pull out the odd coin and then drive over it on the way out. Also check around pay and display' machines.

Historical Information Boards. People gather to read these boards and may drop objects in the process.

Moorland Markers. British moors are littered with ancient stones from megalithic monuments to single stones, for which the original purpose is lost to us. Both the Ancient Britons and the Romans erected marker stones in remote places, the Romans also placing milestones on minor roads running across moors. Anglo-Saxon landowners marked the boundary of their territory with standing stones and replaced many of them with crosses when converted to Christianity.

In medieval times the Church was a major economic force. Monasteries erected crosses to mark the boundaries of their sheep farms and to mark the lines of packhorse routes over the moors. Sanctuary crosses were placed close to churches and chapels whereby an accused person could evade capture and imprisonment by reaching the site of such a cross.

There was a great religious revival in the eighteenth and nineteenth centuries in England and Wales, where hellfire preachers would travel from parish to parish preaching sermons. Where there was no suitable building the congregation would be told to gather at a local cross for the sermon. In some places where local people could not afford a church or chapel, they paid for a preaching cross. Towards the end of the nineteenth century similar crosses were used to mark county boundaries.

Apart from the fact that these crosses would have had people tramping around them for perhaps hundreds of years, they could act as markers for burying of hoards and there is a tradition of leaving money on top of crosses for needy travellers. Paths linking crosses would also repay searching.

Postboxes are often set in grass also letter-boxes at the gates of, usually large, properties.

Postbox and bus stop set in grass verge

Seats and Benches are found in many places, parks, viewpoints, picnic areas, pub gardens, hills, etc. Coins lost while sitting down usually end up behind the bench.

Telephone boxes. A dying breed but any on grass verges would be worth a search.

Toilets. Like at bus stops, looking for that penny to spend will put loose change in the ground. Men and women shaking wet hands to dry them outside can lose rings. I have seen that happen!

Gold and diamond ring

Victorian and Edwardian street lamps, especially those nearest the first and last house in the settlement. As well as being a general landmark for meetings; lovers, in particular, would meet under them.

16 SPORTS

Old newspaper reports, senior citizens and field names will help you track down former sports venues.

Angling is fishing for sport with a rod and line and became fashionable in England in the seventeenth century among the clergy and others who were excluded from hawking and hunting. Any stretch of water which holds or may have held fish is a candidate so as well as looking at modern angling spots where you may be able to search in the closed season you could look for former ponds, lakes and river banks, etc.

Saxon brooch from river bank

Archery. See Military.

Bowls in some form or other has been played since the thirteenth century but was largely banned, in favour of archery, until Tudor times.

There were no real bowling greens until around 1830; any flattish piece of land with, or without grass, would suffice. Wagers were made on the games as with cricket.

Bull and bear baiting were common spectator sports in the seventeenth-nineteenth centuries, taking place generally at bullrings and town and village greens. It was usual to use dogs, one at a time, to attack and defeat the tethered bull or bear; there were also bull versus bear matches. Betting on the best dog or outcome was rife. The sport went into decline by the early nineteenth century owing to being a public nuisance and concerns over animal cruelty. The sport was outlawed in 1835. Look for contemporary newspaper reports of events and riots and mayhem at fairs and wakes.

Church outings. City churches organised outings to rural retreats or chapels with sports fields.

Cock fighting has been around for some 6000 years but was introduced to the West in 1521 through Magellan's voyages. Two cockerels are set at each other in a cockpit surrounded by spectators who bet on the outcome. Some of the birds fought with fitted metal spurs, which were often made of silver. The Cruelty to Animals Act 1835, banned cockfighting in England and Wales but it remained legal in Scotland until 1895. It is still practised in Britain illegally. Look for contemporary newspaper reports of police ambushes of cockpits.

Cricket Grounds. The first reliable reference to Cricket played in England dates to 1550, when it was considered a game for boys. It became and adult game in the seventeenth century and subject to rampant betting on matches in the eighteenth century. When villages without a suitable village green to play cricket on joined the local cricket league, one of their number offered a field on his farm as a possible venue. It was flat, sufficiently wide to allow games to be correctly played, offered reasonable access by footpaths from more than one direction. The Lord of the manor often supplied a cricket pitch as did churches, schools and local businesses.

Cycle racing. There was a boom in 1890s and many sports grounds got perimeter tracks. Famous names attracted large crowds.

Defunct sports venues in the UK. There are hundreds of closed and abandoned sports venues. Here is a great site for those in the UK: https://en.wikipedia.org/wiki/Category:Defunct_sports_venues_in_the_United_Kingdom

Football and Rugby fields. Football is the most popular spectator sport and was first recorded in England in 1409. It has been played in schools since 1581. Rugby developed from football in 1823. Before rules were established, a type of football game called camping was played in some parts of the Country, by as many players who wanted to take part, in many villages up and down the land, every Shrove Tuesday. Early on they used animal (bulls) heads in place of a ball and later an inflated pig's or sheep's bladder. They played on the village green or common or any piece of flattish land nearby. While you probably won't get permission to search Wembley Stadium there are countless sports fields or former sports fields. The Lord of the manor often supplied a sports pitch. Public and Private schools, local authorities and the church in the nineteenth century provided sports fields to avoid hooliganism or sexual precociousness. Church halls often had sports field attached. Commercial organisations provided sports fields for their workers. Clubs outgrow their sports ground and relocate. When searching, most finds turn up around the goal area but don't forget the centre where they toss a coin.

Greyhound Racing. Greyhound racing evolved from coursing, a type of hunting where a dog chases live game such as a rabbit or hare. The first official coursing meeting, then a high-class sport, was held at Swaffham, Norfolk, in 1776. The National Coursing club was founded in 1858 to regulate the sport. Coursing with an artificial hare was trialled in 1876 but it did not catch on until later. During the nineteenth century, coursing became an increasingly working-class sport and at its peak had more than 150 coursing clubs in Britain, some attracting up to 80,000 people. Coursing declined during the twentieth century, notably due to the development of greyhound racing and there were less than 30 coursing clubs in the UK by 2000. The sport, using live game, was outlawed in 2004.

The first modern greyhound race in Great Britain took place at Belle Vue Stadium, Manchester, where seven greyhounds raced round an oval circuit to catch an electrically operated hare in front of 1,700 spectators. In the 1940s there were nearly 300 tracks but now only 22. Attendances peaked to 70 million in 1946 but had declined to two million by 2017.

Horseracing. Known since ancient times, horse racing as we know it today seems to have begun in the sixteenth century and was firmly established in the seventeenth century. As only royalty and nobility could afford the horses it became known as the sport of kings, although plenty of lesser mortals came along to watch and bet on races. Gold sovereigns have been found on the old racecourse at Richmond, Yorkshire. There are 59 race courses presently operating in the UK but many more were established, relocated or closed. See:

https://en.wikipedia.org/wiki/List_of_British_racecourses and James Christie Whyte, *History of the British Turf, from the Earliest Period to the Present Day,* 2 Vols. (London, 1840)

Hunting Lodges. Some deer parks were created under the Anglo-Saxons. The Normans turned large stretches of countryside in England and Wales into royal forests, with hunting reserved for the Crown. Scottish kings and some barons and Church leaders also had forests or chases. Lodges were built on the edge of a forest or in a park to shelter a hunting party as required and also house a permanent warden. The earliest royal lodges were timber-built and protected by a moat. Later lodges were elevated to oversee game movement. The buildings range from a simple tower or grandstand to a substantial mansion. They could be called a stand or standing. Warrener's lodges were built for a warrener, in charge of small game.

As hunting game for food was gradually replaced by fox-hunting for the wealthy and worthies, some hunting lodges were abandoned, while others became country houses. Medieval parks existing around 1600 can be found on Speed and Saxton maps.

Motor and Motorcycle racing. The internal combustion engine is now over a hundred years old and cars and motorbikes have been raced almost as long. Racing events have attracted large crowds of spectators huddled together on the grass surrounding the tracks. There are a variety of racing events such as motor racing, speedway (motorcycles), scrambling, stock car racing, go-kart racing and hill climbs. While Motor Racing and Speedway are still popular today with a huge following, many tracks have fallen into disuse, most likely because they became too small to accommodate the increasing speeds being accomplished.

Prize Fights. Although bare-knuckle fights are recorded from the seventeenth century, the first bare-knuckle champion of England was James Figg, who held the title from 1719 until he retired in 1730. Prize fighting was outlawed from 1750 but it was kept going with royal patronage, fights drawing huge unruly crowds up to 30000 supporters, known as the fancy. Gold guineas were frequently bet on matches. There were also sideshows and thieves. Moulsey Hurst and Crawley Downs were major venues. After several deaths in the 1830s, the authorities increasingly endeavoured to stamp-out bare-knuckle boxing, driving it underground. Fights then tended to be organised in relative secrecy at county boundaries to confound county-run police forces. The last great prize fight in England took place at Sparrows Green, Wadhurst in 1863 although lesser ones are recorded up to 1885. See: Pierce Egan, *Boxiana or Sketches of Modern Pugilism, Containing all the Transactions of Note Connected with the Prize Ring During the Years, 1821,1822,1823,* vols, 1-4, (London, 1824); Henry Downes Miles, *Pugilistica: the History of British Boxing,* 3 vols, (Edinburgh, 1906). Check old local newspaper reports for police ambushes at prize fight venues and attempts by magistrates and civic corporations to prevent crowds gathering at traditional 'sports grounds.'

Pub Outings. City pub landlords organised outings for the faithful to country pubs with gardens and surrounding fields.

Ski Slopes. There are 77 real snow and artificial ski slopes in Britain; the only natural ones being in Scotland. On the other hand if you are visiting overseas resorts there is plenty of opportunity. Objects dropped in soft snow will quickly disappear.

Sledging and tobogganing areas. You do not always need snow, a good frost is sufficient. A sledge run can be very profitable. The rough ride down most sledge runs is enough to lose any coin. Research can lead you to sites which were used during Victorian times or earlier. A talk to elderly friends who remember sledging themselves could be invaluable.

17 TRADING

Boot fairs were apparently introduced into the UK in the 1970s, modelled on the similar Canadian trunk fair. The sales have gained popularity over the years and are held regularly all over the Country, through most of the year. Some are held on tarmac or concrete which can only be searched 'eyes only' of course but plenty are held on fields. As well as recent coinage, other things will have been dropped by buyers and sellers and there may be older finds from the site's history.

Fair Sites. If you wondered how the rich estates came by their wealth, apart from agriculture, a major source of income for the Church and manor was the holding of markets and fairs. One of the most popular early market and fair sites was the village church, cathedral or abbey, where the rents for the stalls went to the priest, bishop or abbot. Early on, stalls were set-up inside the church (worshippers stood for services, so there were no pews until sermons became excruciatingly long in Tudor times) and gradually were pushed out into the churchyard. In 1285, The Statute of Winton forbade establishing new markets and fairs in churchyards and over the next 200 years, many markets and fairs were moved; some owing to eviction by church officials; others because of expanding churchyards taking over the site. Even so the new site would probably still be within sight, or easy reach, of ecclesiastical supervision.

If market and fair rights weren't granted to the Church, they were usually granted to the lord of the manor and consequently the event was held at or close to the manor, where the lord and his servants could keep an eye on the proceedings.

Westminster Fair in the fourteenth century

To whet your appetite for searching fairs and markets, here's a nineteenth century description of Stourbridge fair, which was a 'great fair' (i.e. international) and perhaps, the greatest in Britain:

> "In Cambridge there is a small village called Stourbridge, where an important fair was held, which originated in King John's reign, and became one of the largest in Europe. The booths were planted in a cornfield, and the circuit of the fair, which was like a well-governed city, was over three miles. The shops were built in rows, having each a name, as Garlick-row; there were the cheese-fair, hop-fair, wool-fair, and every trade was represented, together with taverns, eating-houses…this will give you some idea of the extent of these old fairs, and indeed it would have been impossible to carry on the trade of the country without them."

The fair's greatest asset was its location. Stourbridge was accessible from the east by sea and river to the edge of the fair; from the west by Icknield Street; from north and south by Ermine Street or again by the sea and river. As well as goods being brought in and taken out, people had to be moved too. Often there were over 50 Hackney Coaches as well as boats, running people between the fair and Cambridge, night and morning. And the gentry came and went in large numbers using their own transport.

I think we can see from the above description that the single most important consideration in where a market or fair was sited is how the goods were transported into and out of the site. The easiest way of transporting heavy or bulky inanimate goods was by water and very many new markets and fairs were set-up at riverside sites, particularly at river crossings which is why many market towns have a river feature such, as ford or bridge, in their name. The problem of using animal transport overland, aside from poor roads, was that animals, like armies, marched on their stomachs and providing the large quantities of food necessary for anything other than a very short journey was a logistical and expensive nightmare.

Produce with legs was a different matter. Drovers or drivers walked cattle, fowl, horses, pigs and sheep to fairs and markets at an average pace of fifteen miles per day overland. Markets and fairs sprang up where roads and track ways crossed or converged. The drovers would bring in livestock, while other goods would be brought in by hand cart or pack-animal transport. The original roads, such as they were, may no longer exist but may be represented by footpaths or other features. Water was still important as the animals had to be watered and fed but not necessarily at the trading site, itself.

Edward the Confessor penny, 1044-6

You can search on ARCHI UK (https://www.digital-documents.co.uk/) or Google for medieval market and fair sites but, although I say it myself, the most comprehensive guide to medieval markets and fairs in the UK is *Successful Detecting Sites* (Greenlight Publishing). Detectorists who have been lucky enough to search major trading sites, report finding handfuls of medieval coinage, including gold, as well as many interesting artefacts. I have searched a couple of medieval fair and market sites which, although modest, have produced enough interesting finds to fill several finds bags.

18 URBAN SITES

A-Z guides employ large scale modern mapping clearly showing paths, open spaces, gardens; shrubberies and overgrown areas in parks; creeping development on farmland; river and stream banks.

Grass areas on estates. Estates built in the 1950s normally have large amounts of grass in the middle separating two roads or at the side where they form a small children's play area. These were often used for recreation, if the park was too far away. These sites can yield large amounts of coinage, etc.

Housing estates have many original features incorporated. Start your investigation with early Ordnance Survey or topographical maps and plot the old features onto the estate.

Old farm house left standing on a modern housing estate

Older towns. Look for any open spaces around towns where agriculture would have fed the citizens. Old copses probably supplied fuel. Gnarled old fruit trees such as plum and crab apple may have been busy early orchards. Pastures and paddocks were used for cattle and pigs, etc. All accessible footpaths, river and stream banks should be searched, particularly in market towns. Kilns for tiles and bricks were sited outside towns. Pits were filled in with refuse or became ponds and lakes. Medieval craftsman lived on the shores.

Pre-war houses. Owners buried valuables in the garden to avoid loss by bombing or fire during WWII.

Streetcombing is the name given to finding treasures on pavements or sidewalks. Whenever you are out and about on foot, train yourself to look out for valuables lying around. You can even find things when riding a bicycle or in a vehicle but don't get so distracted you end up having an accident. Coins are common finds but also look out for banknotes, jewelry, watches, wallets, pocket books, pens, keys, spectacles, change-purses, mobile phones, cameras, postage stamps, scrap metal…

Scan the ground a few yards in front of you but don't keep your eyes down all the time or you'll likely bump into someone or something so **look up, look down, scan, repeat**. Pay particular attention to edges where objects tend to accumulate particularly at walls, fences and gutters or kerbs. If you are going somewhere then returning, make a circular route to cover more ground, even if it is only walking back on the opposite side of the road.

Car parks are good places to look for losses, the action of getting in and out of cars encourages items to fall out of pockets, which may not be noticed particularly on grass and unmade car parks. Park as far away as you can from where you are going so you have more ground to search. If there are pay and display machines, check around them and the reject tray. In supermarket car parks you may find an abandoned trolley with a coin still in the release mechanism. Many stores have coin sorter machines where rejected coins may have been abandoned. Most people have no knowledge of coins outside of what they can spend.

Coins left at change sorter, including Edward VII silver sixpence, 1906

While you are out and about keep a look out for disturbed soil or dumped topsoil. A careful search of such will often bring forth coins and other valuable finds. I know one smart searcher who found two gold sovereign coins in a loose spoil heap in a public park.

19 VOTIVE SITES

Paganism was the prehistoric religion in Britain although the details are largely unknown except that gifts or votive offerings were made to their Gods. The Romans introduced Christianity, which did not replace Paganism completely. The Anglo-Saxons re-established paganism in the fifth and sixth centuries. Christianity was re-introduced during the seventh century by Catholic missionaries. In 601, Pope Gregory I ordered pagan god images to be destroyed and the temples to be used for Christian worship. By the eighth century, England was mainly Christian and the Church banned paganism. Pagan practices, such as leaving votive offerings persisted until at least the eleventh century, however. Here is my experience of a votive site.

Gold for the Gods. "Hark!" commanded the Arch-Druid. "For it is whispered that Roma is restless and Caesar comes with a great army against us. We must make offerings to our gods that we may fare better than our brothers in Gaul. Go to the sacred grove beside the ring of bright water and give generously. Remember our gods want not the common tin money, only the precious yellow metal will do..."

I slowly unclenched my fist hardly daring to look at the coin that I held in my hand in case I was mistaken. It could have been a trick of the autumn sunlight but I swear the horse winked as it dawned on me that I really was holding the second gold Stater I had dug up in the last hour.

Until last spring this field had been pasture for many years. I had searched the field often, not only because it kept surprising me with particularly interesting coins and artefacts but also because it felt comfortable to be there, even though the bright water had long since become a muddy ditch. Under pasture, identifiable finds dated no earlier than medieval but the plough was to change all that.

Much to my chagrin at the time, the day the field was ploughed and rolled the farmer walked across the field and plucked a gold coin from the ground. "Is this any good?" he asked me later, showing me an immaculate gold Stater in the palm of his hand. "You bet!" I said. "Where on the field did you find it? There might be more!" Once I had the information I almost ran to the field and started searching feverishly. Over the next few weeks I was on that field at every opportunity. With the field's previous finds history, I half expected to be taking the spoils away in a wheelbarrow but my detector remained strangely silent for most of the time. I am probably becoming more selective but the only two finds worth mentioning amounted to an Elizabeth I sixpence and a Scottish groat of David II.

An interesting diversion during the search was the appearance of a badger late one afternoon, fully an hour before dusk. After foraging for a while it suddenly started to run straight at me. I had never seen a badger in the wild and as this one seemed pretty large and fast I didn't know whether to stay or run. Secure in the thought that I had had my Weetabix and suspecting the creature just hadn't seen me, I stood my ground. Five yards from me the badger suddenly stopped, sniffed the air and bolted for a nearby hedge leaving me to get back to the business at hand.

The crop had been harvested for more than a month and I hadn't set foot on the field until the farmer asked why I didn't go and have another look. 'The weeds are knee high,' I thought. 'And what's more, I've already searched every square inch.' The question sounded somewhat rhetorical however, so saying "What a good idea!" I made my way to the field. 'Good idea, indeed!' I thought as I struggled through the undergrowth making my way to the far side of the field where the farmer had found his coin. I eventually reached the spot the richer for one piece of lead and a fly button. As I turned at the field boundary I noticed a relatively clear piece of ground a few yards away and headed for that. Just as I reached the patch a crisp signal stopped me in my tracks. I took out a trowel full of earth to be greeted by a gleaming gold disc lying on top of the little black spoil heap. I knew what it was before I had even picked it up and amazingly within the hour I was holding the second Stater, previously mentioned. It was quite some minutes before I had recovered from the shock enough to carry on detecting. It had taken me 25 years to find my first gold coin a couple of years before; now I seemed to be getting the hang of it. Several hours later with a hammered silver penny added to the haul, I met up with the farmer. "I suppose we'll have to report them," he said. "Mine as well." "Yes," I said. "Even though they were yards apart, they are all a couple a thousand years old and probably went into the ground together. I'll hang out for the fourteen days though in case any more turn up."

Fortuitously I happened to be on holiday and was able to return the next day for another go but the success of the previous day was not to be repeated. I had, however, brought an accessory with me which I was keen to try out for the first time. I have long been convinced that somewhere out there, there is a 'philosopher's stone' that, metaphorically speaking, will turn lead dross into gold. In my search for the 'stone' I came across an obsolete Polaroid camera, the SX70, which is able to photograph the aura emanating from buried gold and it was one of these cameras that I had with me. As sunset approached, for this camera only captures gold auras in low light conditions, I set the camera and stood in the centre of a mentally described circle that encompassed the find spots of the three Staters. I took the first shot of the lower part of the field where I had found the two Staters and then stood staring in disbelief at the developing print as bright yellow streaks formed around the find spots. I turned around and took another shot of the upper part of the field where the first coin had been found and was equally surprised to see five separate streaks develop, fainter then the previous print but definite nevertheless. Quite what these pictures were telling me I didn't have the experience to say, but they seemed to indicate that there was more gold waiting to be found. That night, I sent copies of the photos to Frank, a dowser friend in Dublin, to see what he made of them.

The following day I was back on the field with an arsenal of deeper seeking devices: an 11-inch searchcoil on my Laser, my Goldscan pulse induction detector and my dowsing rod. I selected the Goldscan and set about the field, going over the find spots. I was quite surprised at the quantity of non-ferrous metal that emerged although a little disappointed that none was gold.

Having failed to win the National Lottery again, I had to return to work so it was another week before I was able to revisit the field. During the week, Frank returned my Polaroids annotated with crosses, looking like 'Spot the Ball' entries. Frank had dowsed the pictures and come up with some interesting results. In addition to accurately predicting the find spots of the three Staters already found, Frank suggested a total of seven gold coins, two silver coins and a hoard of gold artefacts which remained unrecovered. The following Sunday, I was delighted to find that the farmer had put out a herd of cattle to graze down the vegetation. Short work they had made of it too! Unfortunately, despite this extra help, and throwing in all the technology I could muster, I was still only able to report three gold Staters to the Coroner later that week.

While I continued searching over the following few weeks, nothing significant turned up until finally the plough returned. As if mocking all my previous effort, half an hour after searching the freshly ploughed field, I was holding Stater number four. The next two sessions produced no precious metal and I was beginning to believe that the field only gave up its gold on the initial search after ploughing or harvesting. Christmas was now upon us and I took some time out to study the dowsed Polaroids. The last Stater I had found was just outside the shot and the predicted finds were scattered randomly over the quarter of an acre. Instead of concentrating around the areas immediately around the previous finds as I had been, I thought it would be worthwhile to investigate the predicted find spots one by one. An hour into the search on Boxing day I recovered Stater number five. At the start of my next search, on the second day of the new Millennium, I was a little perturbed to hear crackling noises in my headphones as I switched my detector on but dismissed it as arcing from an electric fence. It was approaching dusk with almost nothing in my finds bag when I noticed that a piece of brass scrap I had just passed the coil over, failed to produce a signal. I unplugged the headphones and scanned the brass to check the detector, which reassuringly gave a clear signal. I continued detecting expecting to go home with nothing for my foolishness in not spotting the headphone problem earlier, but the gods were forgiving that day for the last signal pointed out a gleaming gold crescent; the edge of Stater number six just breaking the surface.

By this time Bill, the Coroner's Officer, had broken into a sweat over the mountain of paperwork I had caused him and was threatening to attack my detector with a chainsaw. Undaunted I carried on the following weekend and added one more Stater to the score, making the total a magnificent seven.

The development of the crop meant it was time to call it a day. After checking with the farmer that I really wasn't going to be allowed back on the field until after harvesting in August, the Coroner rescheduled the inquest for February.

At the inquest the coins were declared Treasure on the advice of the British Museum whose expert said he considered that the coins were part of a hoard that had been scattered by the plough during hundreds of years of cultivation. I gave my personal view that the coins wouldn't have survived without a scratch had they been subjected to such harsh treatment and that they probably were buried more or less where found, as votive offerings in a place that was a classic contender for a Celtic sacred site. My hypothesis generated some interest but the Coroner went for the scattered hoard theory, not that it matters; for who can say how those coins came to be deposited in that field over two thousand years ago. A further 20 coins have been added to the total since.

Hoard of Ambiani E gold staters, c. 50BC

Potential votive sites.

*Ancient churches, which could have been built on a pagan site.

*Fords.

*Graves. Pagan burials often contain grave goods; Christian burials do not. Known graves will be protected. If you discover human bones cease detecting and report it to the authorities.

*Hill forts. These will undoubtedly be scheduled but surrounding land may not be.

*Lakes.

*Local legends relating to paganism, druids, holy sites, etc.

*Ring of bright water. Bodies of water with an island or islands.

*River Sources.

*Roman bridges.

*Sacred groves especially where oak trees surround a spring or boggy ground.

Druids and Ancient Britons at a sacred grove

*Saint Michael features. The name is associated with votive sites.

*Single Iron Age coin finds. ARCHI UK database is good for this.

*Springs.

*Standing stones but beware of scheduling.

*Trees but only yew, chestnut and oak live long enough to have been around in pagan times.

*Watersmeets where two or more watercourses converge.

*Wells.

Roman rural shrines. These were located close to track ways and usually well away from known settlements. There are seldom any clues to such sites, except perhaps a spring, either running or dried-up. The finds themselves are usually the clue that you have stumbled on the site or one is nearby. Look out for an abundance of rolled or folded lead sheet pieces, Roman coins, (especially minims and pierced coins) and complete or broken artefacts.

20 WASTE

Drain waste. I expect you have seen a sludge gulper vehicle, with a long suction pipe down a drain. They suck up all the rubbish and silt that accumulates in the bottom of drains to keep the drain clear and functioning. Drains are sited at low points so coins and even jewellery dropped nearby are washed or migrate towards the drain and disappear down them frequently. When you see a local sludge gulper driver, ask him where he dumps his load: the site, if accessible, will be a gold mine. (The smell soon dissipates!)

Night soil is a traditional term for human excreta collected from cesspools, privies, pail closets, latrines, middens, septic tanks, etc. This material was removed from the immediate area, usually at night, for disposal mainly as fertilizer. In rural areas such as on farms, the household usually disposed of the night soil themselves on local fields. In urban areas, a night soil collector regularly removed the material to a council depot where it would be sold on to local farmers and spread on fields surrounding towns. Look for routes out of council depots and names such as Carter's lane, black path, manure lane and totter's road. You can find farmers who bought night soil from council meeting minutes, 1850-1930.

Old rubbish dumps. In the 1970s finding and digging Victorian rubbish dumps was a relatively easy way of recovering saleable antique items such as bottles, clay tobacco pipes, dolls heads, earthenware, pot lids and many other collectible items. The easy sites have now largely gone, either dug out or built over, and it requires some effort to find sites that produce the antiques that can collectively be worth hundreds or even thousands of pounds. Organised refuse collection did not begin until the late eighteenth century, and only in London. Everywhere else, until well into the nineteenth century, disposing of household rubbish was a do-it-yourself affair. Some would dig a trench close to home, fill it with refuse, cover it with soil and repeat. Most would find a nearby hole in the ground; a disused well, chalk or clay pit. Rubbish was used to raise river banks for flood defences and tipped into marshland, ponds, old canals, disused mines, ravines, brickfields and quarries or dumped over cliffs. The greatest constituent of household rubbish was coal ash from the open fires and when dumped this produced an ideal habitat for elderflower bushes and stinging nettles. Other clues are broken pottery and glass thrown out by burrowing animals or dispersed by agriculture; cart tracks leading to the site and barge mooring and offloading points.

In London and other cities and large towns initially the rubbish was collected and taken to dust yards where it was sorted by scavengers for recyclable materials, while the valuable ash was sold to brickmakers. This profitable method of rubbish disposal (for the corporations) came to an end in the 1860s as the increasing mountains of rubbish generated overwhelmed the system and the demand for recycled material fell. Brickmakers continued to buy unsorted refuse, which they screened at the brickworks to recover the ash but corporations increasingly resorted to paying contractors to dispose of their rubbish.

Landowners with marshland or a useable hole in the ground profited from selling dumping rights, at least until the site was full. The preferred sites were those accessible by waterway or railway, since barges and railway trucks could carry the large loads necessary.

Probably the easiest method of locating lost Victorian rubbish dumps is to basically look for substantial holes in the ground on nineteenth and early twentieth century maps and check against more recent maps to see if the holes have disappeared. If they have and are not built over then you have a potential early rubbish dump worth investigating on the ground.

When you find a dump, a metal detector search, with permission, will be well worthwhile, as valuable (including gold) coins and metal items can be found. You will need the landowner's express permission to dig it, which may be gained by offering a 50% share of the finds. Equip yourself with stout footwear, 'gardening' clothes and heavy duty gloves; broken glass can inflict serious injury. You only need a few basic tools to dig a dump: a garden fork, a shovel, a T-shaped probe rod for pushing into the surface until you strike glass and a builders pointing trowel to tease out the find once exposed; a rake will also be useful. Bring boxes or buckets and old newspaper to wrap and store your finds. However be aware that dump digging can be dangerous. Never dig alone; always have someone with you, even if they are only watching. Ideally, when starting out, it would be best to join a local bottle club and partner up with an experienced digger who can show you the ropes.

Rag waste. When we wonder how metal objects we find arrived there in the first place, we tend to think they were lost or discarded by people working, resting, playing or undertaking some activity on the land itself. In carrying out research, we may look for places where large numbers of people used a particular area of land for as long a time as possible. But another way metal objects end up on fields is through fertilizer or manure, for it seems that for centuries we have been able to persuade farmers that some of the waste generated by society and industry can be spread on their land to enhance crop production.

One particular waste fertilizer that was used from fairly early times to the latter half of the twentieth century was discarded rags. *The Rural Cyclopedia* of 1849 records that at least 20,000 tons of rags were being annually consumed by the farmers of southern England alone. A contemporary analysis of rag waste stated the metal content was 7.5% by weight, suggesting that over 1,500 tons of metal objects were spread on Britain's cultivated land, every year! This metal was rejected by the industries using rags and consisted of all manner of artefacts either attached to clothing or loose within it, such as buttons, badges, brooches, coins and so on. How did this come about?

Papermaking, which had been developing in Britain since Tudor times, saw the earliest industrial use of rags. The papermakers used rags almost exclusively made from plant fibres, mainly cottons and linens and only white material until the nineteenth century. By 1800, around 500 paper mills in Britain were consuming 11,000 tons of rags annually, to produce a similar amount of paper, by hand! At this point there were insufficient rags being produced in Britain so the shortfall was made up by imports, mainly from continental Europe. In 1803 the first successful mechanised paper machine was installed at Frogmore, Hertfordshire and the demand for rags soared until cheaper straw and wood pulps were introduced in the mid-nineteenth century. Even so there was still a great demand for the higher quality rag based papers, well into the 1960s.

William Bond Wheelwright states in *How Paper is Made,* (1918): "The rags received contain many buttons, hooks and many other hard substances. These are cut off by knives. Buttons abound in the rags and each girl [rag dresser] has in front of her a heavy upright knife like a broad-bladed scythe, which does service in cutting off these buttons." While commentators avoid discussing the fate of these buttons and other metal artefacts, there is a suggestion that some may have been mixed with ash from the mill boilers and there were always unsuitable rags for disposal.

From my personal knowledge of the paper industry, you can be certain that much metal-containing papermill waste ended up being spread on fields, probably with lots of coke as well.

Rag dressing at a papermill

A selection of silver coins probably from waste

The other great user of rags was the shoddy and mungo trade. Up until the beginning of the nineteenth century, woollen cloth was made from 100% pure new wool and Britain had to import wool, mainly from Spain, to sustain the demand. The Napoleonic wars seriously restricted imports, which led to woollen cloth manufacturer, Benjamin Law, developing a method of recycling soft woollen rags with virgin wool to make a new cloth known as shoddy, in 1813. A little later his nephews were able to use hard woollens and tailors' clippings, unsuitable for shoddy, to produce a similar cloth called mungo. Until this time, worn out woollen clothes made of animal fibres, had only been fit for use on scarecrows or dumping on fields as manure. Now discarded clothes were being gathered up from orchards and potato fields to be sold to rag merchants to produce shoddy and mungo. By 1855, the industry, centred on Batley in Yorkshire, was consuming over 15,000 tons of woollen rags annually. Again there was insufficient raw material at home and rags from Hungarian gipsies, German beggars and Russian peasants were imported along with monks' gowns, lawyers' robes, coachmen's jackets, soldiers' uniforms, maidens' bodices and noblemen's cloaks. At various times America and Australia were great sources of rag supply, not to mention Austria, Denmark, Italy, Turkey and most of the civilised world.

In textile production, metal was not only unwanted but any reaching the grinding machine could cause sparks and set the mill on fire! Seams were too thick for the process also, so it was usual to shear off the seams complete with any metal attachments and reject them for use as fertilizer. There was a custom among travellers, particularly soldiers, to either have buttons of silver or gold or to sew high value coins inside seams so that they had a means of buying their way out of trouble if they became stranded. Almost everything attached to or hidden in the seam would have ended up on the land. Consider also the many local militia forces raised during the Napoleonic wars and later disbanded or remodelled into the Territorial Army. Then there were several changes of military organisation and dress, each perhaps requiring a change of buttons and badges. Also many wars have occurred up until the 1950s when shoddy and mungo was finally superseded by man-made fibres. This would have put a very large amount of very collectable and valuable artefacts and military buttons in the ground from redundant uniforms, not to mention coins and civilian dress attachments. For instance early military buttons and volunteer militia buttons can sell for many pounds each, even in dug condition and with shanks missing. Bear in mind also that most fertile arable land would have seen use long before the production of paper, shoddy and mungo so earlier metal objects will also turn up.

How then do we find the last resting places of these artefacts? The set-up seems to have been that most major cities and towns had one or more rag merchants where rags were sorted predominantly into quality and colour. A considerable amount of rag waste was rejected at this stage and sold to farmers. The sorted rags were then transported to the various paper, shoddy and mungo mills, which in turn would generate waste to be used as fertilizer. All the shoddy and mungo mills appear to have been in Yorkshire. Almost every county in the British Isles had at least one paper mill, while Lancashire, Kent and Yorkshire had more than 30 mills each. Transport cost money in earlier times just as it does today, so I imagine that rag merchants and mills would dispose of as much waste as they could locally before sending it long distances by rail or waterway. The destination would depend on where the waste could be sold for most profit. *The Rural Cyclopedia* says that woollen rags are a valuable manure particularly for hops, fruit trees and vines. Kent and adjacent counties are frequently mentioned as recipients of rag waste, while Berkshire, Oxfordshire and other counties are also named, so its use seems to be fairly widespread on arable land, orchards and hop gardens.

To pinpoint rag merchants and mills, we could peruse old trade directories such as *Kelly's*, which should be available at your local library or can be purchased on CD. It is possible that some merchants and mills kept extensive records that may show which farms they sold waste to and these records may be deposited in the County Archives or museums. My favourite approach, however, is to study one of the major agricultural surveys of the twentieth century to find suitable land which may have been spread with rag waste.

The first Land Utilisation Survey of Britain was undertaken in the 1930s by Laurence Dudley Stamp of the London School of Economics. *The Land of Britain* report, published between 1933 and 1948 in ninety-two printed parts, one for each administrative county, describes, in the main, the agriculture of Britain at the time. While there are small black and white thematic maps included in the reports and much of interest, the accompanying specially coloured one inch to the mile (1:63,360) maps based on the Ordnance Survey 'Popular or 4th Edition' are most revealing. Mapping was carried out by volunteers mostly at the scale of six inches to the mile (1:10,560) and although these were never published, they may be available at county archives along with the smaller scale published maps.

The published Ordnance Survey map was overprinted with six basic colours to broadly indicate land-use categories: yellow (heath and moorland), light green (meadowland and permanent grass), dark green (forest and woodland), brown (arable), purple (gardens, etc.) and red (agriculturally unproductive). There are further subdivisions mainly coinciding with detail already on the Ordnance Survey base map. The purple 'Gardens' is divided up into 'houses with gardens sufficiently large to be productive of fruit, vegetables, flowers, etc.' 'orchards' and 'new housing areas, nurseries, allotments and new orchards'. In looking for potential sites of rag waste fertilization the best areas to consider are the purple 'orchards' and the brown 'arable'. New orchards (only shown on some maps) may also be productive but that's less certain than established orchards with good rail or waterway links with London or major cities. This would get the fruit crop to market and make it easy for bulky, heavy rag waste to get to the fields.

Now, while obtaining a suitable original copy of one of these maps for your personal use is extremely difficult, all 168 maps have been digitized and are freely available to study on-line at:

http://www.visionofbritain.org.uk/maps/ Click on the 'Land Use Maps' tab, then 'Geographical Publications Limited Land Utilisation…' and a seamless compilation map will be displayed. Use the navigation arrows or cursor to find the area of interest and zoom in or out to suit. At the bottom of the screen thumbnails of the complete original maps with their keys are shown. You can click on the thumbnail of the map to open it and navigate around that. To print a section of map, use the print screen facility to copy to the clipboard, then paste the map into a photo editor like MS Paint and print from there. Having a printed copy of the map to show the farmer will help your case when you seek permission. Now I appreciate that not everyone has Internet access, so if that is you, take this book along to your local library and they will help you examine and print some of these maps. They may even hold the actual published paper maps.

If you want to do more research you can check out earlier large scale Ordnance Survey maps, produced since the 1850s, and even the earlier tithe maps. This may shed more light on the history of a particular site and the length of potential rag waste usage.

So have another look at your detecting patch and, subject to any necessary permission, try out some of those sites you haven't previously considered. You never know what you may find!

21 WATER SITES

Beach and foreshore. While beaches and tidal river foreshores have seen thousands of years of use for gathering food, fishing and the launching and landing of boats, the seventeenth century saw an upsurge in the number of beach users owing to the practice of sea bathing for perceived health benefits. Following a rise in popularity during the eighteenth century, thousands of people have visited beaches every year to enjoy boating, playing games, sunbathing, swimming, relaxing and having fun. Even today, the majority of families have at least one of their annual holidays on a beach somewhere. Trains, motor transport and the airplane made it increasingly possible for families to travel long distances to resorts and many beaches, particularly in warmer climes, are packed with people all through the summer.

Over the centuries thousands of ships have been wrecked off coasts around the World, particularly off shale and rock beaches where the seas can be very treacherous. Many ships sank with huge quantities of treasure and valuables including Spanish galleons which sank with vast hoards of gold and silver over 400 years ago. Tides, winds and storms often deposit this treasure, particularly gold and silver coins, on the beach. Most modern metal detectors can be used in a couple of feet of water to search for these treasures and there are also metal detectors available especially for searching underwater.

Not only are beaches well visited by people but beach activities positively encourage metal objects to be lost. In hot weather, rings become slightly larger and slide off fingers; in sea-water fingers get smaller and rings slide off. Sun-tan lotion acts as a lubricant, aiding ring slippage, while swimming and frolicking puts a strain on the catches of neck chains and bracelets, which are also frequently lost. One source quotes over 20,000 rings are lost annually, just on British beaches. Most jewellery is never found by its owners. Rarely do people know exactly where they lost anything and even if they did, it is still extremely difficult to find without a metal detector. Jewellery and coins are also lost playing beach games, while trouser and shorts pockets were not designed to safely retain coins and valuables when their wearers are lounging in deck chairs. People going bathing in the sea habitually leave their valuables behind in a towel or removed clothes, then absent-mindedly tip them into the sand when drying off and dressing.

Beach recoveries

Beaches and tidal river foreshores make excellent search areas but you should always be extremely careful when metal detecting and be aware of the ever changing conditions and the high and low tides. Always make sure that you have an easy and pre-planned route back to safety if the tide is rising. Protect your detector from wind-blown sand and spray by fitting a waterproof cover to the control box and other exposed electronic units. You can usually buy manufactured control box covers or get by with elasticized shower caps or plastic bags held on with rubber bands.

You will maximize the amount of beach available and your search time if you arrive, when the beach is not crowded, roughly three hours before low tide. You should then be able to productively search until three hours after low tide. You can best find the state of the tide from local annual tide tables bought very cheaply from angling stores or chandlers. Local coastal newspapers also print daily or weekly tide tables. On the Internet you can just Google tide times with place name and you will be directed to a website like http://www.tidetimes.org.uk which will provide the information. You can also get an App like 'Tides Near Me' for your smart phone or tablet.

The tide cycle, that is the period from one low tide to the next low tide or one high tide to the next high tide, is roughly 12.5 hours. Tidal movement is not even; the water rises or falls fastest at mid-tide and slowest at low and high tides. The range of the tide and by the same token beach coverage and exposure is maximized on spring tides around the time of full moon and new moon and minimized on neap tides around the time of the two quarter moons. Phases of the moon are usually given in tide tables and diaries, pictorially represented as a black circle for new moon, white circle for full moon and either a crescent or a black and white circle for each of the two quarters.

You could use your metal detector anywhere and everywhere on beaches and you will make finds, particularly if you fit the largest search head you can handle on to your metal detector, so you cover the beach fast. There are, however, several areas which may prove more rewarding than others for finding mainly modern losses.

<u>Areas where money changes hands.</u> Deck chair rental points and concession stands like children's rides, food, drinks, ice cream, etc. where people gather or queue, are excellent places to search. The sites of abandoned concession sites will also hold losses.

<u>Bathing and beach huts.</u> Searching the surrounding areas, especially routes from the huts to the beach, can be rewarding and also check out sites of abandoned huts.

<u>Beach steps.</u> Search all around steps leading on to the beach and also underneath any wooden steps. Also look for signs of abandoned steps, which may hold older finds.

<u>Caves and coves.</u> Pirates and smugglers always needed somewhere to hide their loot and the nature of their activities often meant that many would have perished before reclaiming their booty. Thoroughly check caves out slowly and methodically, including floor, ceiling and walls. Take great care when exploring caves: always ensure you check the times of high and low tides and never go into a cave when the tide is coming in.

<u>Cliffs.</u> Cliff faces are subject to constant erosion caused by sun, wind and tide. Centuries old treasures may be brought to the surface after a cliff fall. Some cliffs however, are prone to falls so take heed of any warning notices and keep away. Accessible cliff paths are also worth searching.

<u>Defence works</u> can disturb tons of beach material and bring old finds to the surface. Health and safety may prevent you gaining access while work is going on but be sure to check the beach area when work has finished.

Dunes. Picnicking in sand dunes has been popular for centuries, so check any dunes and the paths leading to and from them, particularly after high winds which have caused sands to drift.

Groynes. Sand and shingle moves along the beach, carrying lost metal objects with it, in the direction that the waves hit the beach by a process known as longshore drift. Wooden walls called groynes that extend from the beach into the sea are built to stop the beach washing away and you will see that the sand or shingle is built up higher on one side of the groyne, where material is deposited by wave action. Above high water people tend to use groynes as a windbreak or back rest. You will find coins and artefacts around groynes both above and below the high water mark.

Harbours and boat moorings. Searching at low tide, you will find many objects lost from the boats and the people on them.

Paths. All accessible paths are worth searching and bear in mind dropped objects may also fall onto the verges of the path, so search these as well. If there are no obvious verges but open land at one or both sides of the path, then search the path and the open land out to at least the equivalent of the width of the path or in other words search an area at least three times the width of the path. The courses of paths often change over time so check old views and maps to see where the paths were.

Piers and jetties. Over the years a great many coins and valuables have fallen through gaps between the wooden planks making up many walkways and will lie under and around the pier. The area around support legs often forms a natural trap owing to eddy currents. Many piers have been partially or totally lost to storms, fires and other causes, so check out the area where piers used to be, which you can find on old maps.

Sea walls. The foot of seawalls and barriers act as collection points for objects thrown up by the tides and also, depending on the type of structure, for objects dropped from above by people walking and sitting. During storms, waves often crash over these defenses carrying metal objects with them, which you may find by checking the areas immediately above the sea walls.

Super tips for beachcombers. Rock pools, high points and other areas where debris, driftwood, gravel, rubbish, seaweed, shells and small stones concentrate, are natural traps. These will also contain coins and other metal objects left behind by the receding tide. Check the rubbish carefully too: rings, especially, are often found trapped in seaweed.

Another type of trap found on some beaches are natural gullies running parallel with the tide line and, on the same beach, there may be several going all the way up the shore. These gullies may be a good many yards in length and vary in width from just a few inches to around a foot in width and depth. As the tides move over these gullies they act like riffles in gold panning, trapping heavy objects like coins and jewellery, being carried up and down the beach.

Bear in mind that the tides grade objects on sand and pebble beaches according to size and weight and you will often find coins of similar size in almost perfect rows. Larger coins and objects tend to be left higher up the beach than smaller.

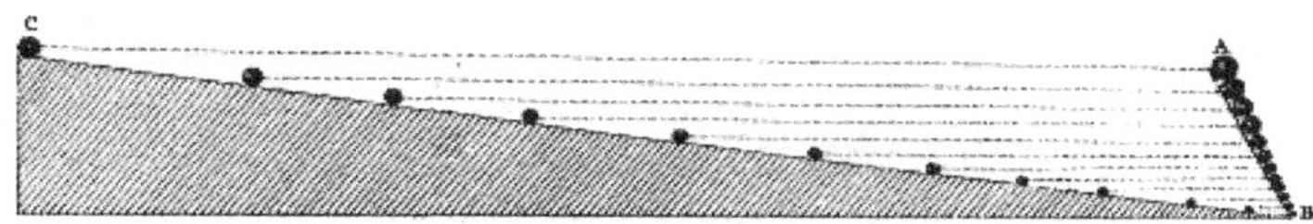

Model showing grading of objects on a cross-section of beach

A great time to hunt on a beach is immediately after a storm with an onshore wind and high seas. Onshore winds can strip beaches down to the hard pack or black sand, where the finds tend to settle naturally. Look out for a definite step formed in the beach around the high tide line: you will find metal objects dropped at the bottom of this step.

When metal detecting on a beach always be aware that you could find other, not necessarily metallic, objects such as wallets, purses, cameras, ship's cargo, relics, wooden chests, credit cards, paper money, books, handbags, binoculars, cell phones, etc. If you find anything that looks remotely dangerous such as oil drums, weapons, ammunition, etc. do not touch but mark the spot and tell the coastguard or police as soon as possible.

The popular beach or resort of yesteryear is not necessarily popular today and it is a good idea to look in the local library, gift shops and book shops for any postcards, maps or local history books showing how the area looked in times gone by. Old photographs, postcards and maps can reveal the sites of vanished piers, moorings, buildings and beach huts. You could also speak to local people, especially the elderly, who may tell you about buried treasure, local legends, smugglers, lost ships and how things used to be. Most of this information will only be stories but you never can tell.

Typical old seaside postcard

Tidal rivers are an especially rich source of coins and artefacts. They are constantly being replenished not only by objects being washed downstream but also brought upstream by the tides from shipwrecks and other items lost at sea and on beaches. Learn as much as possible about the history of the river from the Internet or local library. Of particular interest are old bridges, moorings, buildings, warehouses, tow paths, boat houses, seamen's lodgings, etc. Several tidal rivers also have or had ferry crossings and the hards or landing sites could make good search areas. Shingle patches may be the remains of a ferry or ford.

Invaders used rivers and may have established a beachhead where tidal effect was minimal.

Ask local fishermen and boat owners about the history of the river: there may be tales of buried or sunken treasure and they will also tell you about the multitude of factors than can affect your decision as to where the best search sites might be.

Normally the best places to start searching a tidal river is not only on the river banks but around the 'high spots' that first appear when the tide recedes. As with beaches, these high spots could be real treasure troves. They act as obstructions as the water subsides and all types of debris, junk and rubbish accumulates around them. Amongst the rubbish you will also find what you are looking for.

Case study: finding older losses. Sea charts lend themselves readily to beachcombers. Just as you can go and buy a land map, certainly in coastal parts, you can buy a sea chart. There are two series readily available in the UK: Admiralty Leisure and Imray Yachting Charts. Of the two I prefer the

Imray version which shows drying features (the foreshore) pictorially rather than in abbreviated lettering. In the muddy parts hereabouts, I get more comfort in seeing a patch of stones depicted as dots rather than just the letters 'Sts'. You will have to pay about twice as much for a sea chart as for a land map; they say that a boat is a hole in the water into which you pour money and all associated services conspire to make that a self-evident truth. You can, of course, just stick with your land map, which will show one or two foreshore features such as stones and groynes but you may miss out on other important obstructions or finds traps like jetties, causeways and wrecks.

The area between high and low water is generally where not only jewellery is lost while swimming but also the older losses lie and what's more, the tides refresh the sites almost twice daily. The foot and mouth epidemic, in 2001, well and truly brought the potential of tidal foreshores home to me. On farmland I was finding Celtic, Roman, Saxon, Medieval and modern coins and artefacts, I was relegated to beaches and foreshores by the epidemic and with a little research into maps, charts and local histories, I was coming home with exactly the same range of objects, Bronze Age to modern. So, when all your productive fields are under crop or otherwise unavailable, don't be a stick-in-the-mud, do a little research on any beaches or tidal rivers you can get to and keep bringing home the finds.

Getting back to the foreshore, the first thing I like about stones, or Sts, is the safety factor, if stones don't sink then neither should you. Do be careful though as beaches and river foreshores can be dangerous. Always familiarise yourself with tide times and any local hazards; for example the tide in Morecambe Bay comes in as fast as a horse at the gallop. A few years ago 21 Chinese cockle pickers lost their lives because they were unaware of that fact! Walk out slowly and carefully, if you start to sink, back-up. Carry a whistle and don't venture out onto desolate foreshores without a suitable partner. The second thing I like about stones is that if the tides and currents drop stones, they'll also drop metal objects in the same place, so with safety and finds, it's a double whammy.

I must admit that I am fortunate in living on the coast and within easy reach of three tidal rivers with long histories. We tend to think of Dunwich in Suffolk, England, when we talk of submerged towns and villages but there are a lot more of them. I can name five near me without even trying. There is one that I have been maintaining a watching brief on for some time, which was also a borough and hence had a market. I have recovered a range of coins and objects from Iron Age to modern from there and recently found both an Edward the Confessor penny and a Cnut halfpenny in the same week. There is another large stony area on the same beach, where I found a silver ring of Celtic design, an Edward VII shilling, and other pre-decimal coins. Another spot along the coast where the charts show ancient remains usually turns up something of interest. A friend found a Belgian medieval gold coin there and I have recovered a plain medieval ring brooch and a number of Georgian items including an 1811 one shilling-and-sixpence bank token. Another interesting find was part of a Victorian bracelet featuring a minstrel with a dog.

On the way to my metal detecting club meeting I have to pass a creek running off a tidal river which I thought I would take a look at. The town there is quite historically interesting having possessed a castle and medieval market. I arrived at low tide and looked at the creek first: although it looked stony and firm on the bottom where a trickle of water was running, there were mountains of mud to cross to get there and I thought NO, not on my own. However at the mouth of the creek there is a bit of a beach on the river so I thought I would give that a go. I had only seen the place at high tide before but at low tide it wasn't very picturesque unless you like car tyres, batteries, cans, bottles and bike frames. With some trepidation I went for it anyway. Well it was just nondescript bits of scrap for a while and then I found a George III halfpenny. So I concentrated searching around where I found the coin and found three £1 coins and then a Roman AE3 of Constantine with a good portrait. I found another two £1 coins and a few decimal coppers so it didn't turn out so badly after all.

Another area of beach I've started investigating which interests me is where they used to take horses and carts out to unload the ships and barges, so hopefully there should be old stuff out there. So far I found a lead bag seal marked 1777 (possibly Russian), quite a few decimal coins and the odd pre-decimal coin, including an Australian Edward VII sixpence and a Roman sestertius. I have to say the results have been very encouraging.

Canals. The canal age for industry and agriculture was 1760-1850 but Fens waterways were in use from the fourteenth century. At its peak there were some 4000 miles of canal in the UK. The construction resulted in hundreds of houses being demolished and millions of tons of earth being excavated. Many thousands of labourers were employed who slept overnight in hastily erected camps and drank at the local taverns. You may find these sites through old maps and records. Other areas worth searching are all paths leading from the canals to towns or villages as well as lock gate areas, pub gardens, sites of demolished or abandoned buildings and tow paths.

After the railways took the bulk of traffic, canals were used for pleasure rides and holidaymakers. In the mid-nineteenth century, narrow boats were hired for the day for Sunday school outings. Passenger boats were constructed to carry a large number of people for Victorian day trips and would be towed by 3-4 horses. The towpaths, and stopping places on the routes would be good sites to search. In Scotland, Crinan Canal boats displayed a notice to passengers not to encourage children to run after the boat by throwing money onto the bank and presumably this practice of throwing money occurred elsewhere. Tolls were levied by the canal owners at toll points or toll islands for the carriage of goods and passengers. As with all transport, accidents occurred and boats sank. Charles Hadfield was the authority on UK canals and wrote many books.

Britain still has over 2,000 miles of canals dating from the middle of the eighteenth century. While many waterways have been abandoned, dried up, fallen in to disrepair and perhaps filled in, many others are being strengthened and cleaned to keep them clear of debris, junk and weed and to ensure they remain navigable. Much cleaning and maintenance work is done voluntary, in the UK, by groups such as the Waterway Recovery Group, PO Box 114, Rickmansworth, WD3 1ZY. Tel: 01923 711114. Email: enquiries@wrg.org.uk. http://www.wrg.org.uk, who organise events throughout the main holiday periods, restoring derelict canals. Ask the project organiser if you can use your metal detector along the river or canal bank as well as on the silt and debris removed during cleaning. Always offer at least 50% of the proceeds of any finds towards project funds as money is always required for equipment and transport. See that you actually do the same amount of work as anyone else before using your detector and search at the end of the working day or during rest periods. Here is a list of canals: https://en.wikipedia.org/wiki/List_of_canals_of_the_United_Kingdom

Decoy ponds are known from the seventeenth century and were designed to attract ducks and other wildfowl onto the main pond possibly by installing tame ducks. Several channels ran off the pond, covered in netting. Ducks would be trapped and harvested by being encouraged to travel down one of the channels by a decoyman using a dog or food bait or both. In late Victorian Britain there were around 200 decoys known, a fifth of which were still in operation. See: Ralph Payne-Gallwey, *The Book of Duck Decoys, their Construction, Management, and History*, (London, 1886).

Dew ponds are found in hilly limestone regions such as the Yorkshire Dales, Sussex Downs and Wiltshire. They date back to pre-Roman times and were romanticised by early writers who ascribed them mystical properties. It was often said they were haunted or frequented by witches and a terrible fate would befall the local populace if they dried up. In truth they are, or were, man-made water sources lined with puddled clay. During the sixteenth-eighteenth centuries, larger artificial ponds, many provided with paved bottoms, were constructed in sheep rearing areas and some are still in use. They are often located along ancient drove roads, being used by drovers, shepherds and villagers. Some have run dry but can be recognised by the circular pattern of flat stones. Check aerial photos for patches of bright green grass in hilly areas. Watch where sheep go, as they know where to drink. Edward Martin, *Dew-ponds; History, Observation, and Experiment*, (1914) lists over 40 sites on the South Sussex Downs.

Dredging. Until the railway age, navigable rivers and canals formed the main transport network for the carriage of goods. Dredging was often necessary to keep channels open and the removed silt, containing metal objects, was often dumped near or next to the waterway. Research in local libraries and archives can help you discover if your waterway was dredged and if so, where the silt was dumped.

Lakes, lochs, pools and tarns. Swimming, boating and picnicking took place on and around these waters as did ice-skating, in winter. Check out the shore for losses. If you find an area where finds are concentrated, you may want to check out the water as a potential swimming hole.

Medieval fishponds. Between the eleventh and sixteenth centuries most sizeable manors, monasteries, parsonages and other high-status rural estates operated a construction, for food production, comparable with modern fish-farming.

Man-made fishponds were built from raised banks and earthworks, often providing several linked ponds of considerable size. "Royal" ponds could provide large quantities of fish for the monarch's table, and often were used to stock the ponds of favoured members of the Court. Although early ponds were often rectangular constructions, gradually surrounding land was used to include auxiliary breeding tanks linked by channels and sluices, with different sections for different types of fish. Great Ingenuity was employed in their design, carefully controlled by the design of slopes and sluices.

Many stately homes, maintained extensive fishponds into the eighteenth century, often incorporating them into landscape gardens. Lords of the manor frequently had artificial islands constructed within the larger ponds to attract the growth of reeds and rushes and provide habitat for waterfowl.

Main medieval fishponds were constructed close to any moderately sized river that flowed through the estate, but the majority used minor streams or even springs for their initial water supply. As the external food supply chain developed, these ancient ponds gradually became redundant and neglected, the main dams on which they depended collapsed, but in many areas the basic earthworks still survive, often only as traces, sometimes detectable in aerial photographs or recorded on old maps.

The fishpond would have been a centre of activity, in its time, for the probably numerous manor family, occasional guests, feudal retainers, visiting villagers and poachers who might all have left souvenirs of their presence.

Medieval water meadows. Low-lying water meadows alongside natural waterways were deliberately flooded in wintertime to encourage, normally dormant, grass growth for animal, particularly oxen, feed. Flooding was achieved by damming the water course downstream or diverting water through sluices and channels. There was a shift away from arable to pasture in the sixteenth and seventeenth centuries for sheep farming and more water meadows were created. So water meadows are at least 300 years old and many date back to the thirteenth century.

Moat Sites. There are over 5000 moat sites scattered across Britain dating from the twelfth century. The oldest type are circular. Structures were usually built on the central area, typically a manor house but possibly a chapel, windmill or collection of buildings. Moats were constructed for defence with the added benefit of drainage but they could also be a firebreak in wooded areas or just for show. These sites are almost guaranteed to yield old and interesting objects. Many moats have been wholly or partially filled, remaining undiscovered or unrecognised and may not be scheduled. Examine large scale Ordnance Survey maps as well as aerial and Lidar imagery. Look for groups of ponds in close proximity, especially 'L' shaped ponds, which may have been the corner of a rectangular moat. Isolated circular ponds are probably farm ponds or bomb craters.

Non-tidal water sites. As well as the sea, people have always been attracted to other areas of water such as lakes, lochs, ponds, rivers and streams. Water courses have been used for centuries for bathing, fishing for food, industry, leisure, natural defence, pleasure, powering watermills, transport, washing clothes and as a water supply for drinking and cooking. Since ancient times it has been customary to throw coins and other valuables into water as a thank you for safe passage, an offering to the gods, to make a wish or just for the fun of it. Of necessity, farms and villages have been built around water courses for hundreds of years. Before the advent of swimming pools, thousands of people regularly relaxed by and swam in rivers and streams. Those days have all but gone but the coins and valuables they would have lost, still remain.

The towpath was essential to river transport. Boats could generally sail or paddle downstream but to travel upstream it was usually necessary to tow the boat from the towpath using human or horse power.

Rivers may have changed in width over the years. If the river has narrowed you can assess the original width from the line of trees set back from the present bank. Roads terminating at the waters edge may indicate a port, watermill or waterside inn site. On the other hand it could indicate a point of water supply to a villa or manor house. Trace the road inland to discover where it leads.

Before we talk about searching in water let's think about your safety: people sometimes drown in rivers. Avoid rivers in flood and be very careful when searching in water, especially fast flowing or deep water and particularly where the surface is swirling through eddies or currents. In the water, you should always check the bed in front of you with your detector, digger or scoop to ensure there are no deep holes. If possible take a friend with you or secure yourself, with a length of rope, to a fixed solid object on the bank. There is also the risk of contracting leptospirosis, commonly called Weil's disease, from rats' urine. The infection is commonly transmitted by allowing contaminated water to come in contact with unhealed breaks in the skin, or with the eyes, nose or mouth. Most cases occur in spring and autumn except in tropical areas, where it occurs all-year-round. Flu-like symptoms with vomiting appear after a four to 14 day incubation period. Jaundice, red eyes, abdominal pain, diarrhoea, and rash may also be experienced. I do not actually know of any metal detectorist contracting the disease but it is something to be aware of.

The best way to find objects on the bottom of rivers and streams is to work your way upstream so disturbed silt flows away from you. When you get a signal from your metal detector take a good scoop out the bed and tip it into a plastic sieve. Keep rechecking the hole with your detector and taking further scoops out of the bed into the sieve until you lose the signal, when the object will hopefully be in the sieve. You can make a floating sieve if you obtain a suitable sized car inner tube and lash the sieve into the centre of it. Don't forget to tie the sieve securely to yourself with a suitable length of strong line otherwise your sieve could go floating off and be lost.

Bridges and Fords. Searching the banks and shallow water on either side of bridges would be a good place to start. Apart from such places concentrating people into a small area, there is the possibility of hoards. Check banks and ditches nearby and surrounding fields. Water crossings were often hazardous. The Romans tossed in coins for good luck. Valuables have often been lost or thrown over the side of bridges especially by thieves needing to get rid of loot and weapons in a hurry. The bases of bridge supports act as traps for all manner of debris washed downstream but wherever you find such an accumulation, search thoroughly for coins and artefacts. Where a river or stream is deep or fast flowing, a bridge has probably been there for centuries but not necessarily in the same position. Many old bridges were built of wood and have been either replaced with stone or lost. The sites of old and demolished bridges will be excellent for metal detecting. Where rivers or streams are shallow or slow moving they would normally have been crossed on foot, horseback or carriage by means of a ford. Bridges have replaced most fords but the site of an old ford, which can often be identified by place names containing the word 'ford', is well worth searching. Ancient fords may be dredged.

Items lost beside bridges and fords can move hundreds of yards downstream before coming to rest perhaps in shallow water or near inner curves where the water is very deep and calm. Watch out for eddy currents swirling on the surface of the river, indicating an obstruction on the river bed, which can trap metal objects. Revisit productive areas at regular intervals as they will be replenished as objects are continually washed downstream in a never ending process.

The site of any activity, especially where money changes hands, will result in losses. Check out ferries, hards, landing places, hythes, ports and wharves.

Also check tree roots encroaching into a river or stream as coins and valuables were often hidden in a bag or purse tied to the roots with cord and then submerged. Similarly, check tree branches for old ropes which may indicate the site of a swing.

Over the centuries several shelves can be created in rivers and streams as the water gradually erodes rock and earth. The corners of these shelves can contain a multitude of objects that have been left behind in times gone by. Along with searching the bed, ensure you also search any shelves leading up the bank.

Bridge construction, dredging, droughts and floods are all opportunities for metal detecting. Coins and artefacts that have lain deeply buried for centuries can be brought into detection range. During severe drought certain water courses can dry up completely. Check these out as soon as possible as you may not get another chance for many years.

Dredging operations often result in material removed from the river bed being spread on nearby fields. Similarly, flooded rivers can overflow their banks and distribute their contents in adjacent fields. Rivers in flood can also permanently change course by forming a new cut and many water courses have been intentionally altered by man. Look for these alterations by comparing old and new maps. The former beds and banks could be very productive.

Outdoor swimming. To the Romans swimming in natural waters such as rivers and lakes was an essential skill and the army's ability to swim across lakes and ford rivers helped them create their great empire. Saxons and Vikings, being seafaring people, undoubtedly kept bathing alive until the Christian Church, river baptism notwithstanding, condemned it as ungodly and staying unwashed was believed to ward off disease. Thinking was gradually reversed and swimming enjoyed a revival during the industrial revolution.

The turn of the nineteenth century saw European artists rediscovering the swimming hole. Wordsworth and Coleridge bathed in the Lake District's mountain pools, as Turner, Constable and Ruskin painted a profusion of waterfalls, tarns and ponds, and the fashionable destinations of Europe gave way to the Welsh valleys, Cumbria, the Yorkshire Dales, Cornwall and Devon.

By the 1870s, river and lake-based recreation had become extremely popular. London was expanding exponentially and the population exploited the potential of the Thames watering holes, a cheap train ride away. Edwardian Europe had seen relative peace for a hundred years. Grantchester Meadows on the river Cam became one of the first formal outdoor swimming clubs in the country. Similar clubs, followed at the Cherwell in Oxford. Before long every major public school had its own riverside swimming facilities. At the end of the first quarter of the twentieth century there were more than 600 river swimming clubs holding regular competitions and galas throughout the UK. In our grandparents' day people congregated at swimming holes in summer to swim, paddle, picnic and play.

Post WWII re-development polluted rivers and bathing became all but outlawed for health and safety reasons. Legislation in the 1970s and 1980s improved water quality and over 70 per cent of British rivers are in good or excellent condition and being used again for what is called wild swimming.

Outdoor public swimming pools have been built in Britain since 1815 although the golden age was in the 1930s, when outdoor swimming became popular, and 169 lidos were built across the UK for recreation by local councils. Many lidos closed in the face of cheap foreign holidays but a number of firm favourites remain and recently several closed lidos have been refurbished and reopened.

Some losses will have occurred in rivers and natural waters although most will be on the largely grassed waterside areas where changing of clothes, etc. took place. Ask your grandparents or other seniors where they used to swim. Here are a couple of dedicated websites:

https://www.hungouttodry.co.uk/british-culture

https://www.lidosofbritain.co.uk/

Pump Sites. Prior to piped water supplies, the pump or well in the village was the main source of fresh water and villagers would congregate while waiting their turn to fill up.

Village ponds were essential for supplying water to humans and livestock for centuries and almost every village and farm had one. But as piped water became available many fell into disuse. Over a million have disappeared in the last hundred years and some 400,000 remain. These sites are well worth checking out, especially those beside or served by a footpath.

Waterfalls became the epitome of beauty in the early nineteenth century and became a magnet for swimming, sightseeing and picnicking.

Watermill sites. These mill sites could have been used for centuries and are likely to be rich in old coins and artefacts. If the mill site is unknown just search along the original banks and you will very likely find hot spots where mills were operating.

Mill sites have major potential for metal detecting searches. *The Domesday Book* lists hundreds of mills, and since windmills came later, all the mills mentioned were probably water powered. They were so important as a source of income for their operators, usually the Lord of the Manor or the Church, that mills would sometimes be located on inadequate water sources that only powered them for a few months of the year. Much trading will have taken place at these sites, while the watercourse will have seen considerable human activity for sustenance as well as possible religious, food, leisure and transport uses.

The Domesday survey had no need for maps and most of these, largely wooden, mills will have disappeared, so a little research is necessary to locate them. A few years ago you would have had to pop down to your local library or county archives but nowadays you can do most research on the Internet. If you want to try such research but you are not a computer user, you can easily become one, at your library.

Any post-medieval mill on a watercourse is likely to have developed from a Domesday mill. To get the full picture, we need to consult *The Domesday Book*. There is a free online version: https://opendomesday.org/ or you will be able to look at a printed version at your local library, although, as essential reading for serious medieval researchers, you could get your own copy covering the counties that interest you. The most popular version is published for each county by Phillimore in paperback. If you are interested in more than one or two counties, a cheaper alternative is *Domesday Book: A Complete Translation,* published by Penguin.

Only the total numbers of mills in each manor are recorded as, over 900 years ago, there would have been little need to identify precise locations. This is not a great problem since watermills must have been built on a watercourse of some sort, which reduces the search area considerably. If a half of a mill is listed, the mill probably sits on the boundary with a neighbouring manor, also listing a half, and will be relatively easy to find, as modern parish boundaries often follow those of the earlier manor. Antiquarian, and more recent, local history books and maps, may also be helpful in pinpointing watermill sites. Watercourses may have changed over time, so it is wise to consult old maps and aerial photography to try to determine if there was an earlier course, then follow that to locate your mill and fill your finds bag.

Wells & Holy Wells. Prehistoric settlers located communities near to natural water supplies such as springs, rivers and ponds. The Romans introduced piped water to towns but the source may not be scheduled and can indicate where people gathered long ago. Every castle, country house and farm had to have water supply. Wells became a feature of villages and almost every village green had a well or pump; many remaining in use until after World War I. Some wells were supplied by charity as late as Victorian times amid great celebrations. Thousands of wells are scattered all over the country, from below floorboards in houses to outside castles. Long before the days of running water this was how most people got their water. Some had their own well, while others had to share a communal one, for which they may have had to pay for each bucket of water. Areas surrounding the wells became much used. With these countless journeys losses occur.

For the more adventurous, remember that if a woman put her hand in cold water her fingers would shrink and any rings might become loose. Now, if the ring went down the well it is probably still down there but be careful, toxic gases killed four people in a shaft on Oak Island!

Sacred pools, rivers, lakes, springs and wells abound in Britain particularly in Ancient British areas. Ancient people were fascinated with springs, particularly, and would throw coins and artefacts into the water as offerings to their gods. Look out for water containing islands, the ring of bright water so formed was fascinating to Celtic peoples and the area may be littered with gold coins. Of wells still having names there are probably more than 2000 in mainland Britain. Many are named for Christian saints but are likely to be older owing to the replacing of pagan names with Christian versions. Many pre-Christian deities were female so a well named after a female saint is likely to be old. Some wells are secular named such as Robin Hood's Well, etc. Wishing, cursing and healing wells were activated by a donation, particularly of silver, to the water. Notable wells are probably now inaccessible but the approaches to them offer the best chance of finds. See: Robert Charles Hope, F.S.A., F.R.S.L., *The Legendary Lore of the Holy Wells of England; Including Rivers, Lakes, Fountains and Springs,* (1893) but there are many more wells not listed.

22 BIBLIOGRAPHY AND RESOURCES

Many book and other source references are given in the preceding texts, so I am not going to repeat them here. Just a few that need mention are:

F A Aberg, Ed. *Medieval Moated Sites,* (CBA Research Report No. 17, 1978) https://archaeologydataservice.ac.uk/archives/view/cba_rr/rr17.cfm

ARCHI UK, https://www.digital-documents.co.uk/

Daniel Defoe, *From London to Land's End,* (Cassell, 1888)

Detector User magazine, (1983-4)

Genmaps, http://freepages.rootsweb.com/~genmaps/genealogy/

MAGIC, (land information, e.g. scheduling) https://magic.defra.gov.uk/

Metal Detecting magazine, (1978-80)

National Library of Scotland, http://maps.nls.uk/geo/explore/

Henry N. Shore, *Smuggling Days and Smuggling Ways,* (Cassell, 1892)

The Searcher magazine, (1985-)

Treasure Hunting magazine, (1977-)

John Webb, *The Successful Treasure Hunter's Site Guide,* (London, 1979)

BOOKS IN PRINT FROM THE SAME AUTHOR

THE SUCCESSFUL TREASURE HUNTER'S SECRET MANUAL: Discovering Treasure Auras in the Digital Age, Soft Cover, 230mm x 150mm, (9 x 6 inches) 97 pages, (CSIP, 2016), ISBN 978 1540747815; Hardback, 230mm x 150mm, (9 x 6 inches) 118 pages, (Revised, 2021), ISBN 9798517993397

(Also an E-Book under the title: THE SUCCESSFUL TREASURE HUNTER'S SECRET MANUAL: How to Use Modern Cameras to Locate Buried Metals, Gold, Silver, Coins, Caches…)

CLEANING COINS & ARTEFACTS: Conservation * Restoration * Presentation, Soft Cover, 210mm x 146mm, (8.25 x 5.75 inches) 110 pages, (Greenlight Publishing, 2008) ISBN 978 1 897738 337

(Also an E-Book under the title: THE SUCCESSFUL TREASURE HUNTER'S ESSENTIAL COIN AND RELIC MANAGER: How to Clean, Conserve, Display, Photograph, Repair, Restore, Replicate and Store Metal Detecting Finds)

PERMISSION IMPOSSIBLE: Metal Detecting Search Permission Made Easy, Soft Cover, 210mm x 146mm, (8.25 x 5.75 inches) 78 pages, (True Treasure Books, 2007) ISBN 978 0 9550325 3 0 (Also an E-Book)

SITE RESEARCH FOR DETECTORISTS, FIELDWALKERS & ARCHAEOLOGISTS, Soft Cover, 250mm x 190mm, (9.75 x 7.5 inches) 160 pages, (Greenlight Publishing, 2006) ISBN 1 897738 285

SUCCESSFUL DETECTING SITES: Locate 1000s of Superb Sites and Make More Finds, Soft Cover, 250mm x 190mm, (9.75 x 7.5 inches) 238 pages, (Greenlight Publishing, 2007) ISBN 978 1 897738 306

THE SUCCESSFUL TREASURE HUNTER'S ESSENTIAL SITE RESEARCH MANUAL: How to Find Productive Metal Detecting Sites, (E-Book)

THE ESSENTIAL GUIDE TO OLD, ANTIQUE AND ANCIENT METAL SPOONS, Soft Cover, 210mm x 146mm, 88 pages, (True Treasure Books, 2008) ISBN 978 0 9550325 4 7 (Also an E-Book)

DOWSING FOR TREASURE: The New Successful Treasure Hunter's Essential Dowsing Manual, Soft Cover, 230mm x 150mm, (9 x 6 inches) 96 pages, (CSIP, 2016) ISBN 978-1518766060 (Also an E-Book)

MY ANCESTOR LEFT AN HEIRLOOM: Discovering Heirlooms and Ancestors Through the Metalwork They Left Behind, Soft Cover, 210mm x 146mm, (8.25 x 5.75 inches) 84 pages, (True Treasure Books, 2011) ISBN 978 0 9550325 6 1

(Also an E-Book under the title: MY ANCESTOR LEFT AN HEIRLOOM: Hunting Family History and Genealogy Treasure Through Metal Detecting Finds)

METAL DETECTING MADE EASY: A Guide for Beginners and Reference for All, Soft Cover, 210mm x 146mm, (8.25 x 5.75 inches) 128 pages, (True Treasure Books, 2014) ISBN 978 0 9550325 7 8 (Also an E-Book)

FAITHFUL ATTRACTION: How to Drive Your Metal Detector to Find Treasure (E-Book)

TOKENS & TRADERS OF KENT in the Seventeenth, Eighteenth & Nineteenth Centuries, Soft Cover, 215mm x 140mm, (8.5 x 5.5 inches) 112 pages, (True Treasure Books, 2015) ISBN 978 0 9550325 8 5 (Also an E-Book)

HOW TO FIND BRITAIN'S BURIED TREASURE HOARDS, Soft Cover, 295mm x 210mm, (11.75 x 8.25 inches) 150 pages, (Greenlight Publishing, 2017) ISBN 978 1 897738 627

METAL DETECTING BENEFITS FOR LANDOWNERS, (with Jacq le Breton), Soft Cover, 230mm x 150mm, (9 x 6 inches) 28 pages, (CSIP, 2016) ISBN 978-1537341118 (Put your contact details on the back cover and give to landowners when requesting permission)

TREASURE HUNTING for PROFIT: With and Without a Metal Detector, Soft Cover, 230mm x 150mm, (9 x 6 inches) 220 pages, (CSIP, 2018), ISBN 978 1726407847 (Also an E-Book)

GUIDE TO WHITSTABLE AND ITS SURROUNDINGS 1876 (Illustrated), (W J Cox) Soft Cover, 230mm x 150mm, (9 x 6 inches) 103 pages, (Independently Published, 2019), ISBN 9781794180987 (Also an E-Book)

MANOR HOUSES OF BEDFORDSHIRE PAST AND PRESENT, Soft Cover, 230mm x 150mm, (9 x 6 inches) 102 pages, (Independently Published, 2019), ISBN 9781075574238 (Also an E-Book)

INTERNET SITE RESEARCH FOR DETECTORISTS: How to Find Productive UK Metal Detecting Sites Using the World Wide Web, Soft Cover, 230mm x 150mm, (9 x 6 inches) 75 pages, (Independently Published, 2019), ISBN 9781693198311 (Also an E-Book)

THE SUCCESSFUL METAL DETECTORIST'S SITE AND FINDS LOG BOOK, Soft Cover, 230mm x 150mm, (9 x 6 inches) 249 pages, (Independently Published, 2019), ISBN 9781705335918

A GUIDE TO EUROPEAN COINS 800 BC - 1900 AD, Soft Cover, 230mm x 150mm, (9 x 6 inches) 174 pages, (Independently Published, 2020), ISBN 9798666302606 (Also an E-Book)

THE SUCCESSFUL METAL DETECTING SITE AND FINDS LOG BOOK, Soft Cover, 230mm x 150mm, (9 x 6 inches) 133 pages, (Independently Published, 2020), ISBN 9798669425456

THE SUCCESSFUL METAL DETECTING SITE LOG BOOK, Soft Cover, 230mm x 150mm, (9 x 6 inches) 131 pages, (Independently Published, 2020), ISBN 9798669891527

THE SUCCESSFUL METAL DETECTING FINDS LOG BOOK, Soft Cover, 230mm x 150mm, (9 x 6 inches) 131 pages, (Independently Published, 2020), ISBN 9798669919368

HOW TO RESEARCH FARM HISTORY FOR METAL DETECTING Soft Cover, 230mm x 150mm, (9 x 6 inches) 34 pages ISBN 9798725310764 (Independently Published, 2021) (E-Book, 2020)

METAL DETECTING BRONZE AGE BRITAIN (E-Book, 2021)

METAL DETECTING IRON AGE BRITAIN (E-Book, 2021)

METAL DETECTING ROMAN BRITAIN (E-Book, 2021)

METAL DETECTING ANGLO-SAXON & VIKING BRITAIN (E-Book, 2021)

METAL DETECTING MEDIEVAL AND TUDOR BRITAIN (E-Book, 2021)

ABOUT THE AUTHOR

David Villanueva was born in Birmingham, in 1951. In the early 1970s, Ted Fletcher's book, *A Fortune Under Your Feet*, inspired him to buy a metal detector: a Goldfinger BFO. The performance was very poor by current standards, but it did find coins, and David became hooked. A few months later he upgraded to a deeper-seeking Pulse Induction machine and became very fond of searching beaches, which produced lots of modern coins and jewellery at the time.

Following a move to Whitstable in Kent, David began to search nearby beaches with his trusty old Pulsedec, but quickly found that it was not well-suited to local conditions. He switched to a locally produced C.Scope 1220B, which worked well on the drier parts of the beaches, and this encouraged him to try out some inland sites. He joined the Swale Search and Recovery Club, which he now chairs, and also gained permission to search a small farm, making all sorts of finds that previously he had only read about in the metal detecting press. Having long had a keen interest in history, David started researching his locality, which led to more productive sites to search and to write about in *Treasure Hunting* and *Searcher* magazines as well as a number of published books.

Continually delving into local history and following up his research in the field, David suddenly found himself having to frequently report real treasures in the form of a hoard of Iron Age gold coins, a Bronze Age founder's hoard and Roman, Saxon and medieval gold and silver jewellery.

Made in United States
Orlando, FL
03 December 2024